William H. Pivar
Edward A. Mordini

Power Insurance Letters

A Professional's Resource for Sales Success

Dearborn
Financial Publishing, Inc.

While a great deal of care has been taken to provide accurate and current information, the ideas, suggestions, general principles and conclusions presented in this text are subject to local, state and federal laws and regulations, court cases and any revisions of same. The reader is thus urged to consult legal counsel regarding any points of law—this publication should not be used as a substitute for competent legal advice.

Publisher: Kathleen A. Welton
Acquisitions Editor: Patrick Hogan
Editorial Assistant: Kristen G. Landreth
Associate Editor: Karen A. Christensen
Senior Project Editor: Jack L. Kiburz
Cover Design: David Corona Design

Published by Dearborn Financial Publishing, Inc.

Printed in the United States of America

94 95 96 10 9 8 7 6 5 4 3 2 1

Library of Congress Cataloging-in-Publication Data

Pivar, William H.
Power insurance letters : a professional's resource for sales success / William H. Pivar, Edward A. Mordini.
p. cm.
Includes index.
ISBN 0-7931-0914-0
1. Selling—Insurance. 2. Sales letters. 3. Sales promotion. 4. Insurance companies—Records and correspondence. I. Mordini, Edward A. II. Title.
HG8091.P58 1994 94-2152
368'.0068'8—dc20 CIP

CONTENTS

PREFACE .... **xii**

CHAPTER 1 About Letters **1**

Sales Letters **3**
Asking for Help **6**
Calling after a Letter **6**
800 Number **7**
Testimonials **7**
Lists **7**
Coupons **7**
Color **8**
Cards **8**

CHAPTER 2 Letting People Know **9**

Letter to Friends Prior to Entering Insurance Profession **11**
Note to Friends (Acquaintances) upon Entering Insurance Profession **12**
Neighbor Letter **13**
Letter to Friend/Acquaintance—New Area of Coverage **14**
Letter to Friends, Neighbors and Clients—Change of Affiliation **15**
Letter to Friends, Acquaintances, Neighbors or Former Clients upon Opening Your Own Office **16**

Notice to Friend/Acquaintance on Achievement/Designation/Course Completion 17
Seminar Invitation........18
Offer To Speak........19
Inquiry Made to Chamber of Commerce........20
Office Relocation Notice........21
Open House or Grand Opening Invitation........22
Christmas Season—"Drop By and Say Hello"........23
Holiday Open House Invitation........24
Letter to Clients Concerning a Sale of Agency........25
Purchase of Agency........26
Purchase of Agency Accounts........27
Change in Personnel Handling Account........28

CHAPTER 3 General Insurance Solicitation Letters........29

Insurance Audit #1........31
Insurance Audit #2........32
General Insurance #1........33
General Insurance #2........34
General Insurance—Single Person........35
General Insurance—Career Woman........36
Multipurpose Letter—Auto, Homeowner, Supplemental Health........37
Multipurpose Letter—New Resident........38
Free Coupon........39
Client Referral........40

CHAPTER 4 Life Insurance Solicitation Letters........41

Industrial Life (Burial Life)........43
Term Insurance #1........44
Term Insurance #2........45
Convertible Term Insurance........46
Mortgage Insurance........47
Whole Life Insurance #1........48

Whole Life Insurance #2 49
Whole Life—Children 50
Vanishing-Premium Whole Life 51
Modified or Graded-Period
Whole Life/Recently Married 52
Interest-Sensitive Whole Life 53
Blended Policy (Term/Whole Life) 54
Survivorship Life 55
Survivorship Life Insurance Rates
Response Postcard 56
Universal Life #1 57
Universal Life #2 58
Universal Life #3 59
Low-Load Universal Life 60
Universal Life—Career Woman 61
Universal Life—Single Person 62
Variable Universal Life #1 63
Variable Universal Life #2 64
Split Life 65
Annuity #1 66
Annuity #2 68
Annuity #3 69
Tax-Deferred Annuity 70
Split Annuity 71
Refund Annuity 72
Flexible-Premium Deferred Annuity 73

CHAPTER 5 Disability and Health Insurance Solicitation Letters 75

Accidental Death #1 77
Accidental Death #2 78
Accidental Death—Dangerous Sport 80
Hunter's Life/Disability Insurance 81
Disability Income Protection #1 82
Disability Income Protection #2 83
Individual Medical Insurance 84
Hospitalization Insurance 85

Individual Medical Insurance HMOs and PPOs..........86
Catastrophic Health Insurance..........87
Medicare Supplemental Health Insurance..........88
Long-Term Care Coverage #1..........89
Long-Term Care Coverage #2..........90

CHAPTER 6 Casualty Insurance Solicitation Letters..........91

Auto Insurance—Low-Cost..........93
Auto Insurance—Safe Driver..........94
Auto Insurance—Retiree..........95
Auto Insurance—High-Risk..........96
Auto Insurance—Deal with a Local Agent..........97
Auto/Homeowner Insurance—Deal with a Local Agent..........98
Motorcycle Insurance..........99
Homeowner Insurance—New Purchaser..........100
Expansion of Homeowner Coverage..........101
Homeowner-Auto Combined Policy..........102
Earthquake Insurance..........103
Flood Insurance..........104
Renter's Insurance..........105
Landlord Policy..........106
Umbrella Policy #1..........107
Umbrella Policy #2..........108
Waterbed Insurance..........109
Collector's Coverage..........110
Boat, Snowmobile, Jet Ski Insurance..........111
Home Computer Insurance..........112
Floater Policy..........114
Worker's Compensation—Household Help..........115

CHAPTER 7 Solicitation Letters for Other Financial Products and Services..........117

Financial Planning Solicitation #1..........119
Financial Planning Solicitation #2..........120

Financial Planning Solicitation #3 121
Financial Planning Solicitation #4 122
Financial Planning Solicitation #5 123
Financial Planning Solicitation #6 124
Financial Planning Solicitation #7 125
Financial Planning—New Parent 126
Coupon—Retirement Analysis 127
Attachment to Retirement Planning Coupon 128
Retirement Planning Solicitation #1 129
Retirement Planning Solicitation #2 130
Retirement Plan Maximization 131
Retirement Plan Rollover 132
IRA 133
TSA 134
Estate Tax/Life Insurance 135
College Fundraising Through Estate Planning 136
Charity Fundraising Through Estate Planning 137

CHAPTER 8 Business Insurance Solicitation Letters 139

Business Audit Solicitation 141
Business Insurance (General) 142
Business Coverage (Specific Type of Business) 143
Partnership Insurance 144
Partnership—Disability Buyout 145
Close Corporations—Buyout Insurance 146
Close Corporation—Disability Buyout 147
Inland Marine Protection 148
Business Interruption Insurance 149
Disability Overhead Expense 151
Keyperson Insurance 152
Disability Coverage—Key Employee 153
Professional Malpractice or Business Liability 154
Malpractice Insurance 155
Fidelity Bonds 156
Director's Liability 157
Company Retirement Program 158

Employee Benefit Package 159
Keogh Plan 160
Worker's Compensation Insurance 161
Nonemployee Group Coverage 162

CHAPTER 9 Client Letters 163

Letter after Meeting (Sale or No-Sale) 165
Thank You for Business 166
Service Evaluation Form 167
Transmittal Letter—Requested Data 168
Transmittal Letter (General) 169
Transmittal Letter—Check for Claim 170
Response to Inquiry—Loan/Cash Surrender Value 171
Policy Anniversary Letter 172
Premium Dollars Equal Cash Value 173
Term Insurance Conversion 174
Increase Life Coverage Available 175
Lower Premium 176
Lower Rate Eligibility 177
Increased Coverage—No Premium Increase 178
Increase in Coverage and Premium 179
Modification of Coverage/Renewal 180
Cost-of-Living Adjustment—Disability Income Policy 181
Adding Variable Annuities to a Fixed Annuity Program 182
Dividend Reinvestment 183
Cost-of-Living Adjustment Rider 184
Disability Income Rider 185
Accidental Death Benefit (ADB) Rider 186
New Product (Letter to Present Clients) 187
Renewal Discussion 188
Letter to Former Client upon Failure To Renew 189
Appointment for Physical 190
Acceptance/After Physical 191

Rated Applicant 192
Refusal of Application 193
Cancellation Notice 194
Cancellation—Nonpayment of Premium 195
Cancellation/Refund of Prcmium 196
Notice of Nonrenewal 197
Collection Letter #1 198
Collection Letter #2 199
NSF Check 200
Thank You for a Referral 201
Request for Testimonial Letter after Claim Settlement 202
Request for Testimonial Letter/Check Transmittal Letter 203
Thank You for Testimonial Letter 204
Letter to Client on Newspaper Article about Client 205
Client Birthday—Financial Planning 206
Client Birthday 207
Client Marriage/Engagement 208
Birth of Son/Daughter 209
Sympathy 210
Christmas Card 211

CHAPTER 10 Letters of Conflict 213

Policy Holder Complaint 215
General Complaint—No Solution 216
Complaint—Full Settlement 217
Complaint—Settlement Offer 218
Release of Claim 219
Complaint—Recommendation to Insurer 220
Complaint—Offer To Arbitrate 221
Answer to Complaint—Legal Inquiry 222
Forward of Complaint—Legal Inquiry to Law Firm 223
Official Inquiry—Complaint 224
Complaint Resolved 225

CHAPTER 11 Carrier Correspondence 227

Carrier—Request for Representation 229
General Transmittal Letter..230
Status Inquiry...231
Complaint—Payment 232
Low Claim Offer...233
Letter to Carrier—Claim Denied/Recommendation..234
Complaint—Failure To Take Action 235
Carrier—End of Relationship...................................236

CHAPTER 12 Employee Letters...................................237

Employee Transmittal Memo 239
Notification of Meeting 240
Notification of Training..241
Notice to Agent of Missed Meeting 242
Complaint Follow-Through......................................243
Commission/Expense Dispute..................................244
Employee Congratulations..245
Employee Recognition/Training Completion or
Professional Designation 246
Employee Termination..247
Decline To Hire...248
Employee Birthday 249
Letter of Recommendation 250
Employee Wedding Anniversary 251
Birth of Son or Daughter 252
Employee Anniversary with Firm.............................253
Death in Agent's Family...254
Death of Agent/Employee 255

CHAPTER 13 Press Releases..257

Transmittal Letter to Media.......................................259
Course Completion...260
Professional Designation 261

Sales Award 262
Promotion/Appointment 263
New Agent 264
New Coverage/Representation 265
New Owner 266
Office Opening/Relocation 267

Epilogue 269

Index 271

PREFACE

If you were to analyze your correspondence for the last year, you would likely find that the majority of the letters you sent were similar in content. Nevertheless, you may have devoted valuable time to individually preparing these letters.

One aim of this book is to save you that valuable time by making available to you a series of letters that will fit most of the repetitive business situations you face. Another aim of this book is to maximize the effectiveness of your communications so that your letters achieve the goal for which they were created. By using the table of contents, you will be able to quickly locate applicable letters that clearly convey the intended message. We have also included a large number of direct mail letters to sell specific products or to solicit a meeting with a prospective client. These sales letters are really advertising pieces.

The authors would like to thank Bradley Pivar, who worked on the sales letters. He is the son of one of the authors and a professional advertising copywriter in Los Angeles.

Chapter 1

About Letters

The letter is an ancient form of communication that originated with the earliest written symbols devised by humankind. A letter is simply a written message, and as such it is essential that it accurately convey what the writer intends to say. In letter writing, the KISS rule applies—Keep It Simple and Sincere. In other words, your letter should follow these guidelines:

- Get to the point quickly.
- Use clear and concise language so that readers will not get a message other than the one intended.
- Avoid material that distracts from or obscures the primary message.
- Be honest.

You may be great at working crossword puzzles because of your extensive vocabulary, but remember that the purpose of your letters is to communicate, not to impress.

Business letters are likely to be read by people who are as jealous of their time as you are. Therefore, the message must be quickly understood. If the reader is not getting the message within the first 15 seconds, chances are good that your letter needs to be rewritten.

Sales Letters

Sales letters are different from business letters. A sales letter is really an ad, which is simply a request for business. In advertising, the acronym AIDA is often used. It stands for Attention, Interest, Desire, Action. A sales letter should meet these criteria: it should get the reader's attention, create an interest, create a desire for the product (or more information) and result in either action by the recipient or an anticipation of your call.

The letter must grab the reader's attention in the first few sentences. Once you have the reader's attention, the entire letter will generally be read, even an extremely long letter. Attention-getting headings can be directed to particular interests of the recipient, or they can even be absurd or humorous statements. A heading must, however, lead quickly to a message of interest; if not, your letter will be discarded. Keep in mind that people want benefits and they must be told quickly that benefits are what you are offering them.

In the insurance field you must keep in mind that the letter is generally a tool to get you through a door. Although the letter prepares the reader, letters never sell major insurance products. That is up to you.

All sales letters are not equally effective in getting the reader's attention. Some letters have phenomenal results, while others fail to generate anything other than mailing expense. Because direct mailing is one of the most costly advertising media, in terms of cost per contact, you don't want to waste dollars for mailings that fail to maximize results. Your letter copy is important, and we have provided you with various copy choices. However, copy effectiveness will vary regionally and among target audiences. We therefore suggest that you test your market using different copy so that you can concentrate on what is working most effectively for you.

To evaluate effectiveness you can use specially marked coupons or individual suite numbers as return addresses (never use box numbers, because people don't like sending anything to an impersonal box). A very simple test is to send different mailing pieces to people with last names beginning with different letters. Keeping track of the volume of pieces mailed and the number of resulting appointments or sales will provide a success percentage.

Here are some general do's and don'ts of mail advertising.

Do's

1. Use stationery that clearly indicates that you sell insurance.

2. Your mailing should promise a benefit to the recipient.
3. By indicating in the letter that you will be calling, you more than double the effectiveness of the letter. The reader must give consideration to your message.
4. Personally address all correspondence. Never write "To Occupant." Occupants don't buy, but real people do.
5. Address each letter so that it looks personal to the recipient. Handwritten is best, but not always practical. The letter itself should also be personalized, using the recipient's name. With the aid of a computer, this is a relatively simple task.
6. Target letters to those likely to be interested in the product presented. By using such marketing aids as mailing lists and reverse directories for areas whenever possible, you can use a rifle approach rather than a shotgun approach, in which much of the shot misses the mark. For example, if you are mailing a solicitation for hunters' accident and disability insurance, you should consider mailing to people within your service area who purchased hunting licenses during the previous year. There are many firms that offer specialized mailing lists or can tailor a list to meet your needs.

Don'ts

1. Don't attempt to deceive the reader into believing that you are offering anything other than insurance products.
2. Don't use a postage meter, third-class mail, a stick-on address label or a window envelope; you don't want the letter to look like junk mail.
3. Don't disguise yourself by making your mailing appear to be an official government letter or a check. Doing so is unethical, and you want to establish yourself as a professional, not a sleazy operator.
4. Don't use undersized envelopes that require an awkward fold to the letter.

Asking for Help

When you are writing to a person with whom you are acquainted, you should consider using something like this:

> I will be calling you in a few days asking for your help. I would greatly appreciate any favorable introductions you can provide to your friends and neighbors who might benefit from the services I have to offer.

Most people want to help other people, so the recipient of the letter will likely give some thought to possible referrals and be receptive when you call.

Calling after a Letter

Except for a few very low-cost products, you should not expect to sell insurance on the telephone. What you want from the telephone call is a meeting where you can make a sale.

Here are some general rules about using your follow-up calls:

- ✓ Immediately identify yourself and tie your call in with your letter.
- ✓ Give minimal information about a policy or program. The more information you give over the telephone, the less will be your chance of obtaining a face-to-face interview.
- ✓ Get information. Ask questions. Answering questions with questions is a good technique to consider.
- ✓ Don't ask for an appointment. Instead, set a time and date to meet the prospective client(s). You will generally want both parties present when dealing with couples. Use an option of two positive choices, not one of not meeting with you. "Would you [and Mrs. Smith] be available at 7:30 this evening so I can tell you more about this program, or would 8 PM be more convenient?"

800 Number

Telephone response will diminish if your mailings are outside local calling areas and you are asking the recipient to call you. Even when you tell people they can call collect, the telephone response to your letters will be far less than if the call were in a toll-free zone.

Consider obtaining an 800 number for mailings outside local calling areas. People will make 800 calls with little hesitation. You can either have your own number or use a secretarial service number. Several services will take messages for about $1 per message plus a monthly fee as low as $10.

Testimonials

Testimonials are very effective and can be included as supplements in mailings. If the reader can relate to the person giving the testimonial, by being in similar circumstances or from the same area, for example, the effectiveness of the testimonial is increased. To obtain testimonials, you need only ask. Satisfied clients will generally respond favorably to such a request. Several examples of written requests are included in Chapter 9, "Client Letters." Ask permission to use their names. Adding names is far more effective than just initials, which many people use on testimonial letters.

Lists

You will see that many of the letters in the book contain lists of items identified by a bullet (•) or check mark (✓). Lists are very effective in solicitation letters and *are* read.

Coupons

Coupons are good letter enclosures. Although many agents claim they are not applicable to insurance, they can be effectively used.

One agent included a coupon for one of the best motorcycle helmets available. The coupon entitled the recipient to a helmet at about half the normal retail price if the recipient would complete a request for a no-obligation quote on motorcycle insurance. Because the helmet had to be picked up at the insurance office, it gave the agent a chance to meet the person and ascertain other needs. Incidentally, the agent simply made a bulk factory purchase at a direct price and resold the helmets at cost.

Coupons can similarly be used for children's car seats, auto first aid kits and other safety-related items. Some offices use a coupon for a free windshield sunshade (with "Need Assistance" on one side and the name of the agent and agent's firm on the other side).

Color

Color attracts attention and can be effectively used in flyers and attachments, but letters themselves should appear personal. Color makes the letter appear to be a mass market piece; this can create a negative impression in selling insurance, which is viewed as a professional product. A light color such as buff or gray can, however, convey a professional image. Continued use of a particular color will serve to identify you immediately to your clients as the sender.

Cards

Enclose or attach your personal card with every letter.

Chapter 2

Letting People Know

Letter to Friends Prior to Entering Insurance Profession

[*Date*]

____
____
____

Dear ____________:

I am considering [*a career in*] [*making a career change to*] [*financial planning*] [*the insurance profession*]. It is an important decision for me, and I would appreciate any advice you can provide.

I will be calling you in a few days to set up a meeting so that you can discuss this career with me.

Best regards,

____

NOTE: *This letter is on personal stationery. The meeting you are setting up is not to sell; it is to have your friend play a role in your career move. You should be positive in presenting the career choice. At a later date, when you are selling products, your friend will likely feel some obligation to you both in giving referrals and as a future client.*

Note to Friends (Acquaintances) upon Entering Insurance Profession

[*Date*]

____
____
____

Dear ___________:

I have decided to [*make a career change to*] [*make a career in*] [*financial planning*] [*insurance services*].

I am excited about the products and services that I can offer.

I will be calling you in the next few days to arrange an opportunity to show you the kind of work I do and to ask your help in identifying anyone you know who might benefit from my services.

Sincerely,

____

Neighbor Letter

[*Date*]

____
____
____

Dear ____________:

I am your [*neighbor*] [*new neighbor*] [*at 2716 Lorimer—the white house on the corner*].

I am a [*financial services representative*] [*agent*] [*general insurance representative*] with [*Clybourn & Sons Insurance Agency*]. I wanted to share with you the kind of work I do, as I may be able to answer any questions that are of concern to you about [*insurance*] [*retirement planning*] [*financial planning*].

Sincerely,

____

NOTE: *Add this handwritten note: "I will call you in the next few days to discuss any present or future needs you might have."*

Letter to Friend/Acquaintance — New Area of Coverage

[*Date*]

____
____
____

Dear ____________:

Just a short note to let you know I am now able to meet your needs for [*auto*] insurance as well as [*life insurance*]. I am able to protect you with [*automobile policies*] through [*United Prudential*], [*a variety of companies*] to fit your individual needs [*at the lowest cost*].

I will call you in a few days to get some basic information. This will help me provide protection information for you to consider when your present coverage expires.

[*Very sincerely*] [*Your friend*],

____

Letter to Friends, Neighbors and Clients—Change of Affiliation

[*Date*]

____
____
____
____

Dear ____________:

Just a short note to let you know that I am [*now affiliated with Webster Insurance*] [*now a representative of Strong Hands Insurance*].

I have made this change in order to better serve the [*life insurance*] [*pension planning*] [*total insurance needs*] of my clients. I am very excited about this move and the products that I am now able to offer.

I will be calling you in a few days to say hello, tell you about my service and determine if [*there is any way in which I can serve your needs*] [*you know of any of your friends who might be interested in what I can do for them*].

Sincerely,

____

Letter to Friends, Acquaintances, Neighbors or Former Clients upon Opening Your Own Office

[*Date*]

____
____
____

Dear ____________:

Guess what! I took the big step! [*No, (not marriage), (I am already married*).] I have opened my own office (see letterhead). I am now an [*independent insurance agent representing some of the finest companies in America*] [*independent agent representing* __________________].

I am very excited about the move. I can offer my clients [*a full range of financial and estate planning services*] [*full service for their insurance needs*].

If you are in the area, stop by for coffee and a "hello!" I will call you in a few days asking for some help. I want to tell you about the kind of services I offer that may be of benefit to anyone you may refer to me.

Sincerely,

____

NOTE: Asking for help is an excellent approach to use for a person you are acquainted with. Although it is not directly mentioned in the letter, your telephone call should go beyond requesting referrals—you want to handle the recipient's coverage as well.

Notice to Friend/Acquaintance on Achievement/Designation/Course Completion

[*Date*]

____
____
____

Dear ___________:

[*Just a short note to let you know that I am now entitled to use the (CLU) designation next to my name. This designation stands for (Chartered Life Underwriter), and it denotes special training and achievement few (life) agents ever obtain. I feel that the additional training I have received has better equipped me to provide professional services and advice.*]

[*Just a short note to say I have been made a member of (Washington Life Insurance Company's 100 Roundtable). This award is based on the fact that I was one of the top 100 agents in our state in life insurance sales in 1994. This award is particularly gratifying because it means that I was able to serve the insurance needs of a great number of people who have placed trust in my judgment.*]

I will be calling you in a few days to [*discuss any current or future insurance needs you might have.*] [*ask for your help. I would appreciate any referrals you can provide as to friends of yours who might benefit by my services.*] [*I also want to thank you for your confidence in me in the past.*]

[*Sincerely*] [*Your friend*],

____

Seminar Invitation

[*Crestwood Insurance Services*]
Invites You To Attend A Free Seminar On
[*Creative Estate Planning*]
[*Creative Financial Planning*]
[*Financial Planning In Today's Market*]
[*Retirement Planning*]
Featuring
[*Mr.*] [*Ms.*] [*Michael Jordon*]
[*Nationally Known Author and Financial Consultant*]
10 A.M.
Hyatt Grand Champions Hotel - Crystal Room
Indian Wells
Refreshments RSVP 340-8041

NOTE: *An RSVP gives the invitation an "exclusive" appearance, which generally results in greater attendance than if the RSVP were not included.*

Offer To Speak

[*Date*]

____
____
____

Dear ____________:

I understand that, like all service organizations, you are constantly in need of speakers. Well, I would like to volunteer.

I have prepared a [*30-minute*] presentation on [*The Advantages of Living Trusts*] [*How to Keep Uncle Sam's Hands off Your Estate*] [*Charitable Giving Can Make Dollars and Sense*], which I feel will be of interest to most of your members.

I would be happy to discuss my presentation with you. [*If you are interested, please call me.*] [*I will be calling you in a few days to ascertain your interest in this presentation.*]

Yours truly,

____

NOTE: *Your chamber of commerce should be able to give you a list of local service organizations and persons to contact.*

Inquiry Made to Chamber of Commerce

[*Date*]

____
____
____
____

Dear ____________:

On behalf of [*Mutual Insurance Company of Alabama*] and the [*Charlotte*] Chamber of Commerce, I would like to thank you for the interest you have shown in [*Charlotte*]. Once you have lived here you will realize why so few of our citizens want to live anywhere else.

Should you decide to make the [*Charlotte area*] your home, I hope you will call on me regarding your insurance needs. Our office is conveniently located in the [*Upland Shopping Plaza*], [*just west of Kmart*] at [*1137 Upland Drive*]. We pride ourselves on our personal service and our ability to obtain quality protection. I think you will be pleased with our area rates for [*auto, home, health, life and business insurance*].

Please let me know if there is anything I can do to assist you in your proposed move or any additional information you might desire about our community. I have enclosed a stamped, self-addressed envelope for your convenience if you desire any help or information.

Sincerely,

____

NOTE: *If you are a member of your local chamber of commerce, it will provide you information on inquiries it receives.*

Office Relocation Notice

[*Date*]

____
____
____

Dear ____________:

In order to better serve the needs of our clients, we [*have moved*] [*will move*] our offices to [*1624 West Main*], just [*west of Savon Drug*].

[*We have been in our new office since* ____________.][*We will be in our new office as of* ____________.] The new location offers easy access and parking [*as well as more space*].

I hope the move [*has not*] [*will not*] cause you any inconvenience, and I look forward to continuing to serve your needs. [*I will call you in the next few days to go over your current coverage and to see whether any modifications are needed.*]

____

NOTE: *This letter to policyholders can give you a logical opportunity for coverage review.*

Open House or Grand Opening Invitation

[*United Insurance Agency*]
Cordially Invites You to Our
Open House
[*922 West 52nd Street*]
[*(619) 346-3660*]
[*Wednesday, February 6*]
[*5–8 P.M.*]
Come visit us in our new offices
[*Your Name Here*]
Refreshments Will Be Served

NOTE: *This invitation should be on an invitation card stock. A variation on an Open House would be*

Grand Opening
Of Our New Offices
At

Christmas Season—"Drop By and Say Hello"

[*Date*]

____
____
____

Dear ____________:

When you are in our neighborhood stop by for a [*free Christmas calendar, coffee, cookies and gossip*]. [*If you ask Ellen, she might even go to the closet and bring out a new coffee mug for you.*]

If you can't come by, we send you our wishes for a Happy Holiday Season!

The best to you and yours,

____

Holiday Open House Invitation

[*United Insurance Agency*]
Cordially Invites You to Our
Holiday Season Open House
[*922 West 52nd Street*]
[*Friday December 23rd*]
[*(619) 346-1852*]
[*5 – 7 P.M.*]
Please Come and Visit With Us
[*We Even Have A Gift For You*]
[*Your Name Here*]
Refreshments

NOTE: *Invitation should be on regular invitation card stock.*

Letter to Clients Concerning a Sale of Agency

[*Date*]

____
____
____

Dear ____________:

[*After ____ years, I am retiring from business.*] I am selling the [*Henderson Insurance Agency*] to [*Joan Williams*]. [*Ms. Williams*] will continue with the agency under the [*Henderson Insurance Company name*] [*the name Joan Williams Insurance*].

[*Ms. Williams*] is a dedicated and caring insurance professional who will continue to meet your insurance needs. I am certain you will be very pleased with the manner in which she handles your [*homeowner's*] and [*automobile*] insurance coverage.

[*Ms. Williams*] will contact you in a few days to get acquainted and ascertain any specific needs you may have and answer your questions.

I have enjoyed working with you [*these past nine years*]. I feel I am leaving you in good hands.

Your friend and former agent,

____

NOTE: *This letter should be under the former agency's letterhead.*

Purchase of Agency

[*Date*]

____
____
____

Dear ___________:

My name is [*John Smith*] and I have recently purchased [*Johnson Insurance*]. [*The name is being changed to Smith Insurance.*]

We will, of course, continue to service your [*Homeowner Policy No. 677J38 with United Prudential Insurance Company*].

I will be contacting you within the next few days so that I can have the pleasure of meeting you to review your insurance coverage and answer any questions you may have.

I look forward to meeting you and to meeting your future needs.

Yours truly,

____

Purchase of Agency Accounts

[*Date*]

____
____
____

Dear ____________:

My name is [*Thomas Smith*] and I am the owner of [*Insure All, Inc.*]. Our firm will be handling your [*Homeowner Policy No. 67J371 with United Fidelity*], which was previously serviced by [*Hendricks Insurance*].

I will be contacting you in the next few days to answer any questions you might have. I look forward to the pleasure of meeting you and the opportunity to review your insurance coverage.

Yours truly,

____

NOTE: *By meeting with clients personally, you will reduce the percentage of accounts you will lose to other agents when policies come up for renewal.*

Change in Personnel Handling Account

[*Date*]

____
____
____

Dear ____________:

Just a short note to introduce myself. I am [*Jane Martin*] and I work with [*Johnson Insurance*]. I have been assigned the responsibility for your [*homeowner and automobile*] policies and service.

If you have any questions or problems, I am the person to handle them for you. I look forward to a long and pleasant relationship. [*I will be calling you in a few days to review your present coverage and to ascertain whether any modifications are indicated.*]

Yours truly,

____

NOTE: *Don't mention that your predecessor has left the firm or any other reason for the change.*

Chapter 3

General Insurance Solicitation Letters

Insurance Audit #1

[*Date*]

____
____
____

Dear ____________:

An Important Phone Call Is Coming

In a few days I will be calling you to discuss a no-cost-no-obligation audit of your family protection coverage.

This will include:

- ✓ Auto coverage
- ✓ Special coverage for boats, motorcycles, snowmobiles, ATVs, etc.
- ✓ [*Homeowner*] [*tenant*] protection
- ✓ Special coverage for jewelry, artwork, furs, collectibles, etc.
- ✓ Extended liability protection
- ✓ Health and accident protection
- ✓ Disability protection
- ✓ Retirement and investment savings
- ✓ Business coverage [*if applicable*]

Our computer printout will show the coverage you have and the recommended coverage. If you are not adequately protected, I will be happy to consult with you in meeting your needs.

Sincerely,

____

NOTE: *What you want from this letter is a meeting in order to determine the person's present coverage. For the second meeting, you will make your recommendations, if applicable.*

Insurance Audit #2

[*Date*]

____
____
____

Dear ____________:

A Million-Dollar Dog Bite

It isn't as strange as it seems. Juries have been awarding plaintiffs multimillion-dollar awards for dog bites, slip-and-fall injuries, emotional shock and even injuries sustained by trespassers. Court awards often exceed the defendant's insurance limits.

I will be calling you within the next few days to offer you a no-cost, no-obligation family audit of your insurance coverage. I will provide you with a computer printout showing your present coverage, as well as any areas of risk exposure.

I will also provide costs for any recommended coverage should you desire the additional protection.

Sincerely,

____

General Insurance #1

[*Date*]

____
____
____

Dear ____________:

Ever Worry about Life's "What Ifs"?

What if little green men take your mother-in-law away in their flying saucer—but she's wearing your jewelry?

What if the police recover your stolen Mercedes—but it's painted purple and has rabbit-skin upholstery?

What if your letters to your pension plan come back "Moved—left no forwarding address"?

I'm in the What If business. I can protect you and your family against most of life's What Ifs. I will call you in a few days to find out what your What Ifs are and show you how you can be protected.

Sincerely,

____

[*A full-service independent insurance agent*].

General Insurance #2

[*Date*]

____

____

____

Dear ____________:

Are You:

Naked?

Are Your Assets Exposed?

If you want to be able to say,
"I've Got It Covered!"
Call Me Today for Your:

- *Auto*
- *Home*
- *Life*
- *Business*

Lowest Rates — Personal Service

I Can Cover Them

- *Auto*
- *Home*
- *Life*
- *Business*

at a cost far less than you imagined.

I will call you in just a few days to ascertain your specific needs.

____

General Insurance—Single Person

[*Date*]

____
____
____

Dear ____________:

Single People Need Protection

I specialize in meeting the [*complete*] insurance needs of single men and women.

- Automobile
- Homeowner's Coverage
- Renter's Coverage
- High-Dollar Umbrella Coverage
- Special Coverage for Collectibles and Jewelry
- Health and Disability Coverage
- Business and Professional Insurance
- Retirement Planning

I can offer you personal and caring service with greater coverage, and likely save you dollars as well.

I will be calling you in a few days to ascertain your specific needs so that I can prepare a proposal for your no-obligation consideration.

Yours truly,

____

General Insurance—Career Woman

[*Date*]

____
____
____

Dear ____________:

Career Women Need Protection

I specialize in meeting the [*complete*] insurance needs of career women.

- Automobile
- Homeowner's Coverage
- Renter's Coverage
- High-Dollar Umbrella Coverage
- Special Coverage for Collectibles and Jewelry
- Health and Disability Coverage
- Business and Professional Insurance
- Retirement Planning

I can offer you personal and caring service with greater coverage, and likely save you dollars as well.

I will be calling you in a few days to ascertain your specific needs so that I can prepare a proposal for your no-obligation consideration.

Yours truly,

____

Multipurpose Letter—Auto, Homeowner, Supplemental Health

[*Date*]

____
____
____

Dear [*Mr.*] [*Mrs.*] [*Ms.*] ____________:

I Can Save You Money

If you are [*a safe driver*] [*in good health*] [*a nonsmoker*] [*retired*] [*a senior citizen*], I should be able to show you significant savings on your [*automobile insurance*] [*homeowners' coverage*] [*supplemental health insurance*].

I will be calling you in the next few days to set up a brief appointment. I hope you will be able to spare a few minutes of your time, because it will be to your financial benefit.

Yours truly,

____

NOTE: *As you can see, this simple letter can be tailored to get an appointment for a variety of insurance products.*

Multipurpose Letter—New Resident

[*Date*]

____
____
____

Dear ____________:

Welcome to [*Crestville*]

This is a [*town*] [*city*] [*village*] [*community*] I love and it is where I do business. My business is in meeting people's [*insurance*] [*financial planning*] needs.

If having a local agent available who understands your specific needs and will work to meet those needs at the lowest possible cost is important to you, you will want to talk to me.

I will be calling you in a few days to discuss any present or future needs that you may have.

Yours truly,

____

NOTE: *The chamber of commerce or local welcoming organization can supply you with information on new arrivals.*

Free Coupon

[*Date*]

____
____
____

Dear ____________:

My name is [____________________] and as a way of introduction I have something you can use. It won't cost you a cent and there is absolutely no obligation on your part. Just bring this letter to my office for a

> FREE! Auto Sunshade!
>
> A folding heavy-duty sunshade that
>
> lasts for years, protects your car
>
> and keeps your interior cool.

The sunshade has our firm name on one side, which helps us. On the other side is "Need Assistance," which is to be used to help you in emergencies. After all, that is what insurance is all about—providing for life's emergencies.

Yours truly,

____

NOTE: *By receiving the letter back, you have the names of people who came to your office for the sunshade. Chances are they will be more receptive to you as to subsequent mailings and telephone inquiries than the general public. In addition, coming into your office has made it a familiar place to them. If they need additional services, they are more likely to go to a familiar place than an unfamiliar place (drop-in business).*

Client Referral

[*Date*]

____
____
____

Dear ____________:

Our mutual friend [*Charles Johnson*] [*Carol Jones*] suggested that I contact you.

As you may know, [*Charles*] has been very pleased with what I have done for him as to [*his*] [*her*] [*business insurance*] [*financial planning*] [*homeowner and automobile coverage*].

I will be calling you in the next few days to obtain some general information so that I can present you with a proposal that [*will delight you and make the IRS very unhappy*] [*should save you some serious dollars*] [*meet your specific needs at a sensible cost*].

Yours truly,

____

Chapter 4

Life Insurance Solicitation Letters

Industrial Life (Burial Life)

[*Date*]

____
____
____

Dear __________:

Worried about [*Funeral Costs*]?

For just pennies a day you can have a [*$4,000*] [*burial life policy*].

Interested? [*Call me at 779-3281.*]

[*Complete the enclosed application and send it to me in the postage-free envelope for a no-obligation rate quote.*]

Yours truly,

____

NOTE: *These low-price policies are still common in some Southern communities as well as in some large cities. They are popular with older low-income persons so any mailing should be tailored accordingly.*

Term Insurance #1

[*Date*]

____
____
____

Dear ____________:

At age [*27*], [*$100,000*] of term insurance only costs $____________ per month plus:

- *Coverage is guaranteed renewable until age* [*80*].
- *Double indemnity for accidental death, paying up to $200,000, can be included for only pennies a day.*
- *The policy can be converted to Whole Life Protection up to age* [*70*].
- *If you are disabled, premiums are waived.*
- *You may qualify for a nonsmoker discount.*

I will be calling you in a few days to tell you more about this affordable plan.

Yours truly,

____

NOTE: *Tailor the letter to the product you are offering. From mailing-list information available, you will be able to calculate monthly premiums based upon actual age of addressee.*

Term Insurance #2

[*Date*]

____
____
____

Dear ____________:

Are you interested in [*$50,000*] of additional life insurance for only pennies a day?

It sounds like term insurance and it is, but not all term insurance is the same. We can offer you:

[✓ *A guaranteed renewable policy to age (75)*]

[✓ *Level premium for (five) years*]

[✓ *Conversion privilege to cash value whole life to age (52) without proof of insurability*]

[✓ *Your insurance premium is waived in the event of disability. Applies to age (60)*]

[✓ *Accidental death benefits that (double) (triple) the amount of coverage*]

[✓ *Premiums that adjust with your age, offering young families maximum coverage at lowest cost*]

I will be calling you in a few days to obtain some basic information in order to give you an accurate quote based on the dollar figure you choose.

It costs nothing to listen, and it could mean a great deal for you and your family.

Yours truly,

____

Convertible Term Insurance

[*Date*]

____
____
____

Dear ____________:

I know you have seen the offers of:

$100,000 of Life Insurance
Only Pennies a Day!

This is term insurance, which provides younger people maximum insurance protection at the lowest cost while they are young. However, increasing premiums make this coverage a poor long-term investment.

There is an alternative. It is called

Convertible Term

It provides for:

- ✓ Low-cost protection now.
- ✓ Guaranteed convertible to a number of options [*regardless of any health problems you may develop*].

Options available include insurance protection with cash and loan value, as well as various retirement related plans that also protect your family.

I will be calling you in a few days to provide more information about the advantages of convertible term.

Yours truly,

____

Mortgage Insurance

[*Date*]

____
____
____

Dear ___________:

Congratulations on the purchase of your new home. I wish you and your family many years of enjoyment. However, there will also be many years of home payments. How can you make certain your family will be able to keep your home if you are not with them?

With Mortgage Insurance

your home loan is paid in full should you die. [*In the event of disability, your insurance payments are waived.*]

What Does It Cost?

Probably less than the cost of a pack of cigarettes each day. I will be calling you in a few days to get some basic information so that I can give you an accurate, no-obligation quotation for your protection.

It costs nothing to listen, and it could mean a great deal for your family.

Yours truly,

____

Whole Life Insurance #1

[*Date*]

____
____
____

Dear ____________:

Certificates of Deposit Are a Poor Investment

With low interest rates, a good CD investment will barely keep up with inflation.

WANT SOMETHING BETTER?

An investment offering:

1. Safety
2. Higher yields
3. Liquidity—the ability to borrow on or cash out your investment
4. Tax-deferred and tax-free benefits

PLUS:

You receive insurance protection for your estate that far exceeds your investment.

It's not an exotic untried financial product. In fact, it's been around a long time. However, the likely continuance of low interest rates make it the best game in town.

I will be calling you in a few days to set up an appointment to show you why WHOLE LIFE INSURANCE is the answer to your protection and investment needs.

Yours truly,

____

Whole Life Insurance #2

[*Date*]

____

____

____

Dear ____________:

Can You Live on Social Security Income?

I'm certain you can, but you may have to find a small apartment, clip coupons, watch for sales, stay well and stay home.

But Is That Really Living?

If you want to be able to travel, vacation, entertain friends and make the most of your retirement years, you'd better have something going for you besides Social Security. What I would suggest is:

A Plan for Living

There is a product for living with guaranteed annual growth at a rate you won't match today at your bank. When it's time to retire, you can convert to a choice of annuities that will supplement your retirement income. As an added benefit, you will receive high-value insurance protection until you annuitize the policy.

I will be calling you in a few days to get some basic information so that I can prepare a no-obligation proposal that can mean gold to you in what are called the golden years.

Yours truly,

____

NOTE: *With certificate of deposit rates low, whole life insurance has become a very attractive product.*

Whole Life—Children

[*Date*]

____
____
____

Dear __________:

Life Insurance for Children—Why?

Well, there are a number of reasons why thousands of parents are buying life insurance for their young children. They include:

- Setting up a savings plan for college, marriage or ?
- Locking your children into permanent insurance rates that will never be lower
- Guaranteeing insurability now when future jobs or health could make insurance costly or impossible to obtain

I will be calling you in a few days to tell you how little it costs for a high-yield whole life policy of $25,000 or even more.

Yours truly,

____

Vanishing-Premium Whole Life

[*Date*]

____
____
____

Dear ____________:

Thinking Ahead to Retirement?

Certainly insurance plans make sense, they provide interim family protection plus provide savings at a favorable rate of interest,

But:

How can you make the premium payments when your income is decreased after retirement?

There Is an Answer:

A vanishing-premium plan that lets you adjust a program for your specific needs. The payments can stop when you retire.

The advantages:

- ✓ Faster-growing cash value.
- ✓ At retirement you have a paid-up policy with all value and benefits intact.

Does It Make Sense to You?

I will be calling you in a few days to tell you more about vanishing-premium whole life protection.

Yours truly,

____

Modified or Graded-Period Whole Life/Recently Married

[*Date*]

____
____
____

Dear ____________:

As a recently married person, you probably feel that you need but can't afford whole life insurance.

That may have been true a few years ago, but now we are able to offer you a [*modified-premium*] [*graded-premium*] whole life policy with significantly lower premiums for the first [*five*] years.

[*Want more information and a free quote? Fill out the enclosed information card for a no-obligation rate quote for the coverage you choose.*]

[*Want more information? I will be calling you in a few days to tell you more about this special plan and to get some basic information so that I can prepare a no-obligation quote for a policy to meet your specific needs.*]

Yours truly,

____

[*Enclosure*]

Interest-Sensitive Whole Life

[*Date*]

____

____

____

Dear ____________:

What Insurance Policy Do Insurance Professionals Choose for Their Families?

- Fixed low premiums
- Savings that increase with interest rates
- Use of the interest to pay premiums
- Guaranteed cash value
- Guaranteed death benefits
- Income tax benefits

When I call you in a few days, I will provide information about a fantastic new investment and insurance plan that accomplishes all of the above and more.

Yours truly,

____

NOTE: *Interest-sensitive whole life goes by a number of names, such as "current-assumption whole life" or "excess-interest whole life."*

Blended Policy (Term/Whole Life)

[*Date*]

____
____
____

Dear ____________:

I Didn't Believe It Either!

[*$100,000*] worth of life insurance for not much more than the daily cost of a hamburger and a Coke. Especially a policy that offers:

- Steadily building cash value
- Paid up additions
- Premiums that stay the same
- On-demand borrowing power

But It's True!

By combining features of whole life insurance and term insurance, we are able to offer a plan that will very likely meet all your protection needs at a premium that makes sense.

Want to know more? I will be calling you in a few days to get some information so that I can give you a no-obligation quote.

Yours truly,

____

Survivorship Life

[*Date*]

____
____
____

Dear ____________:

First the Bad News:

Estate taxes are here to stay. If there are any changes, we can expect them to increase what the government takes. This means that Uncle Sam's share will significantly reduce the size of the estate that passes to your survivors.

Now the Good News:

There is a solution: a relatively new concept called survivorship life. This insures a husband and wife jointly on the same policy. It allows for significantly lower premiums even when one spouse has health problems. It is a plan designed to take care of your estate taxes when due.

[*Interested? Well, I will be calling you in the next few days to provide you more information about the advantages of survivorship life.*]

[*Interested? Well, I will provide a computer worksheet showing costs with no obligation on your part. Simply complete the information on the enclosed post card.*]

Yours truly,

____

Survivorship Life Insurance Rates Response Postcard

Please send me rates on [survivorship life] insurance.

Name: ______________________________

Address: ______________________________

____

My Date of Birth: ______________________

My Spouse's Date of Birth: ______________

Also provide me with information on:

- ☐ Estate planning
- ☐ Tax shelters
- ☐ Living wills
- ☐ Low-cost term insurance
- ☐ Charitable remainder trusts
- ☐ Disability benefits
- ☐ Long-term care benefits
- ☐ Universal/variable life
- ☐ Investment programs
- ☐ Spouse insurance

Universal Life #1

[*Date*]

____
____
____

Dear ____________:

They say the only two things in life that are certain are death and taxes.

They Are Only Partially Right!

There are little-known provisions of the tax code that the IRS would prefer you not know about.

It's possible to:

- Allow your interest income to compound without paying taxes until withdrawn.
- Keep interest income tax-free if paid as a death benefit.
- Allow you to withdraw and spend insurance premiums that you have paid without any tax liability.
- Purchase life insurance using untaxed interest earnings.

I will be calling in the next few days to show you how you can accomplish all of the above and even more. Of course, it is not going to please the IRS.

Yours truly,

____

NOTE: *This letter is aimed at obtaining an appointment to discuss a universal life package. While interest rates are low, universal life programs are not necessarily an attractive investment. A whole life policy would likely better meet a client's needs. However, as interest rates rise, this approach can be effectively used.*

Universal Life #2

[*Date*]

____
____
____

Dear ___________:

What gives nightmares to the IRS?

It's the Last Great Tax Shelter

While it may seem too good to be true, your attorney and accountant will agree that it's perfectly legal.

I will be calling you in a few days to arrange to provide you more information about an insurance plan that will keep your dollars where they belong, in your pocket and not with the IRS.

Yours truly,

____

Universal Life #3

[*Date*]

____
____
____

Dear ____________:

You Can Still Beat the IRS

Universal Life is the tax collector's biggest nightmare!

- Interest earnings are tax deferred until withdrawn.
- Interest earnings may be tax-free when paid as a death benefit.
- Your premiums paid may be removed from the policy tax-free before taxable interest earnings.
- Life insurance protection is purchased with untaxed interest earnings.

Don't you believe it when others tell you the days of tax shelters are gone. I will be calling you in a few days to show you what a custom-designed Universal Life program can mean to you in terms of income, protection and, best of all, tax savings.

Yours truly,

____

Low-Load Universal Life

[*Date*]

____
____
____

Dear ____________:

Consumer Reports calls this:

"The Best Kept Secret In Insurance"*

It's the policy that most insurance carriers don't want to sell because it gives most of the profit back to the policyholder.

Interested?

I'll be calling you in a few days to tell you more about costs, coverage and, best of all, the significant tax benefits that this policy offers.

Yours truly,

____

**Consumer Reports*, August 1993.

NOTE: *This is a letter for a low-load Universal Life Policy.*

Universal Life—Career Woman

[*Date*]

____
____
____

Dear ____________:

Are you interested in a retirement plan designed for the:

Career Woman

We understand the particular needs you face and have a program that makes it possible to:

- Allow your income to compound without paying taxes until withdrawn.
- Keep interest income tax-free if paid as a death benefit.
- Withdraw and spend insurance premiums that you have paid without any tax liability.
- Purchase annuities using untaxed interest income.

I will be calling in the next few days to show how you can accomplish all this and a great deal more. Of course, it's not going to please the IRS.

Yours truly,

____

Universal Life—Single Person

[*Date*]

____
____
____

Dear __________:

Are you interested in a retirement plan designed for:

Single People

We understand the particular needs you face and have a program that makes it possible to:

- Allow your income to compound without paying taxes until withdrawn.
- Keep interest income tax-free if paid as a death benefit.
- Withdraw and spend insurance premiums that you have paid without any tax liability.
- Purchase annuities using untaxed interest income.

I will be calling in the next few days to show how you can accomplish all this and a great deal more. Of course, it's not going to please the IRS.

Yours truly,

____

Variable Universal Life #1

[*Date*]

____
____
____

Dear ____________:

Want Investing Flexibility?

- Want to save for retirement with a tax-deferred investment?
- Want to invest in the stock or bond funds you choose?
- Want to be able to borrow on your earnings?
- Want to be able to withdraw invested capital while leaving your profits to increase?
- Want to be able to pass your investment on to your heirs tax-free?

You can do it all with an amazing product called variable universal life.

I will be calling you in a few days to provide more information about a plan that can provide you with the financial security and flexibility you want.

Yours truly,

____

Variable Universal Life #2

[*Date*]

____
____
____

Dear ____________:

Interested in a No-Lose Investment Plan?

- ✓ Highly profitable investment.
- ✓ A fixed annual cost.
- ✓ Pay no taxes on the profit.
- ✓ You choose how the profits are reinvested.
- ✓ If you should die, your family will get everything back you paid plus a whole lot more.

What's this miraculous investment called? Why, it's [*Variable Life*] [*Variable Universal Life*].

I will be calling you in a few days to tell you more.

Yours truly,

____

NOTE: *Letter can be tailored for an individual variable plan you are offering.*

Split Life

[*Date*]

____
____
____

Dear ____________:

Why Give Till It Hurts?

When you can give the same amount or even more with relative ease.

Split Life

is a way to make sizable charitable contributions at bargain basement prices. It's the chance to give thousands, hundreds of thousands or even millions of dollars to the charity of your choice at a cost so low you will think it can't be true.

I will call you in a few days to provide you more information about split life and to determine whether the plan fits in with your planned charitable giving.

Yours truly,

____

NOTE: *The above letter is for a policy of term insurance coupled with an annuity. The insured customarily makes a gift of the high-cost annuity portion to the charity while keeping the lower-cost term insurance portion. The insured continues to make payments on the whole policy, but that portion covering the annuity is a tax-deductible gift.*

Annuity #1

Low CD Rates?

Afraid Your Money Will Run Out
Before You Do?

There Is A Better Way

SENIOR ANNUITY PLAN

Guaranteed by [*Mutual of La Crosse*], this plan will maximize your monthly income.

> **Example:** At age 76 a [*fifty thousand dollar*] investment will give you:
> [$807] Per Month For Life
> **Plus:** You or your heirs are guaranteed the return of your investment.

I will be calling you in a few days to tell you more about this amazing plan.

Yours truly,

____

NOTE: *This would be a good mailer in a more affluent retirement area.*

As an alternative last paragraph, consider the following:

Want more information? Complete the following and send it to me in the enclosed postage paid envelope for a no-cost-no-obligation computer worksheet prepared to meet your personal needs.

Name ________________________________ Age __________

Name of Spouse ________________________ Age __________

Amount of funds that you would be able to invest in a lifetime senior annuity: $ ___________

Address ____

____

Telephone __________________

Annuity #2

[*Date*]

____
____
____

Dear ____________:

Could You Use [*$2,000*] Extra Each Month?

When added to your other retirement benefits, [*$2,000*] each and every month could mean the difference between subsistence living and enjoying your retirement years.

I will be calling you in a few days to demonstrate how easy it is to ensure financial security for your future (plus provide protection for your family). Remember, the only thing that waits for you in the future is what you send on ahead today!

Yours truly,

____

Annuity #3

[*Date*]

____
____
____

Dear ____________:

Question: What's the difference between a retired gentleman and a bum?

Answer: A paycheck

An additional check for $1,000, $2,000 or more each and every month can make a big difference in your retirement years.

I will be calling you in a few days to demonstrate how easy it can be to ensure financial security for your future [*plus provide family protection now*].

Yours truly,

____

NOTE: *Annuity letters such as this could also be used for whole life coverage.*

Tax-Deferred Annuity

[*Date*]

____
____
____

Dear ____________:

Like to Play the Stock Market?
Want an Absolutely Secure Investment?

Whatever you like, you can have, within the envelope of a

Tax-Deferred Investment Annuity

- You pick the investment fund.
- Transfer from one fund to another without charge.
- No sales charges.
- Pick your own payout options.
- Provides for automatic dollar-cost averaging.
- Guaranteed death benefits.

Interested? I will be calling you in a few days to demonstrate why a Tax-Deferred Investment Annuity is the best thing to come along since sliced bread.

Yours truly,

____

Split Annuity

[*Date*]

____

____

____

Dear __________:

It's Here!

The Best of Two Worlds!

A split annuity that provides:

1. Guaranteed fixed return
2. A variable annuity that can be invested in a variety of mutual funds

I will be calling you in a few days to tell you why a split annuity makes sense in today's economy. A few minutes of your time could mean a very profitable and secure future.

Yours truly,

____

Refund Annuity

[*Date*]

____
____
____

Dear ____________:

Worried about Retirement?

Let me show you about the no-gamble annuity plan that offers:

✓ A guaranteed minimum annuity.

✓ Should you die before the full recovery of your annuity fund, your estate shall receive the remainder.

✓ And there is more.

I will be calling you in a few days to discuss your needs so that I can prepare a no-obligation proposal tailored to those needs.

Yours truly,

____

Flexible-Premium Deferred Annuity

[*Date*]

____
____
____

Dear ____________:

Expecting an Income Tax Refund?

You can spend it now and it will be gone forever, or you can:

Invest in Your Future

A [*single-premium annuity*] can mean:

- ✓ Immediate cash value
- ✓ Tax-deductible loan value
- ✓ Tax-deferred investment benefits
- ✓ Insurance benefits for premature death
- ✓ Guaranteed income for life

Like to know more? I will be calling you in a few days to provide you with more information about this opportunity and to answer any questions you may have. Remember, the only thing that waits for you in the future is what you send on ahead today!

Yours truly,

____

Chapter

5

Disability and Health Insurance Solicitation Letters

Accidental Death #1

[*Date*]

____
____
____

Dear ____________:

Think You Can't Afford Life Insurance?
How About
[*$250,000*] Life/Accidental Death
At Only [*38¢*] Per Day

What's the catch?

It's quite simple: at your age your most likely cause of death would be an accident. While an ordinary life policy in the amount of [*$250,000*] would likely cost more than you can presently afford, you can easily afford an accidental death policy that protects you against your greatest peril.

I will be calling in a few days to arrange to meet with you [*and your spouse*] to discuss this program, as well as programs you should consider for the future to [*ensure your children's education*] and [*your retirement*].

Yours truly,

____

NOTE: *For mailings consider using marriage license registrations for the past five years, which are a matter of public record. You can also buy mailing lists of married couples by age category.*

Accidental Death #2

[*Date*]

____
____
____

Dear __________:

Are You a Traveler?

When you fly, do you pop quarters in the airline insurance machine? For only [*$*__________], probably less than you're spending in quarters, you can have

[*$250,000*]

in accidental death [*and disability protection*] covering accidents in

1. Scheduled airlines
2. Taxis, buses and trains
3. [*Private autos*]
4. [*List other coverage*]

For [*immediate coverage*] complete the enclosed application and mail it with your check for [*$*__________] for [*one full year's*] protection, or charge it to your Visa or MasterCard.

Yours truly,

____

Enclosure

Traveler Insurance

Name______________ Age ____ Telephone ________

Address ______________________________________

City ________________ State ______ Zip __________

Please provide me with [*$250,000*] of [*Traveler's Insurance*] [*accidental death insurance*] covering death related to [*accidents involving scheduled airlines, taxis, trains, buses, private auto*].

Name(s) of my beneficiary(ies): ____________________

____

Address ______________________________________

☐ Enclosed is my check for [*$97.50*] to cover one year's premium.
☐ Please charge one year's premium [*$97.50*] to my:
☐ Visa ☐ MasterCard

No. __________________ Exp. Date ______________

____
Signature

Accidental Death—Dangerous Sport

[*Date*]

____
____
____

Dear __________:

I know you will be interested in:

Sky Divers' Insurance

[*$1,000,000*]

Life Insurance
For Accidental Death
From Accidents While Sky Diving
Only
[*$36/Month*]

Call Now For Immediate Coverage

1-800-368-4293
Charge to Visa or MasterCard

[*I will call you in a few days and answer any questions you might have about this amazing insurance protection. Incidentally, you can charge the premium to your VISA or MasterCard.*]

Yours truly,

____

NOTE: *The identical approach can be used for skin divers, spelunkers, hang gliders, bungee jumpers, etc. Use membership lists of clubs for mailings. Leave flyers wherever equipment for the sport is sold.*

You will find that married high-risk-sport-activity participants are a relatively easy sale, since insurance tends to relieve some of the guilt of participating in what could be a dangerous hobby.

Hunter's Life/Disability Insurance

Hunter's Insurance

[*$250,000*] Accidental Death
From Gunshot or Arrow

[*Hospital and Disability Coverage*
From Gunshot or Arrow Injuries
See Policy or Contact Agent for Coverage]
Only

[*$39.50*]/ Year

Call ______________

[*(717) 347-3660*]

Charge to Visa or MasterCard

NOTE: *This flyer can be used as a letter or included with other mailings. Flyers can also be left at sporting goods shops and wherever hunting licenses are sold.*

It would also be a good handout at an outdoor activity show.

While a low-cost product, it offers an entry for additional client coverage.

Disability Income Protection #1

[*Date*]

____
____
____

Dear __________:

Did you know that

Nearly 1 Out of 3

people become disabled for 6 months or more before reaching the age of 65?

Disability Income Protection

starts when your paychecks stop. It replaces lost income from disability due to sickness or accident. The cost:

Pocket Change

based on daily cost. [*Call me today and I will prepare, at no cost or obligation, a proposal based on your income.*]

[*I will be calling you in a few days so that I can prepare a no-cost, no-obligation proposal based on your income.*]

[*Jane Smith*] Insurance

1-800-673-7200

Disability Income Protection #2

[*Date*]

____

____

____

Dear ____________:

Question: What's Your Most Valuable Asset?

Answer: It's Your Ability To Earn Income.

No matter where you work or what you do, the continuity of income is of vital importance to you.

Sure, you have life insurance, but to collect you have to die. The basic facts are that at age [*32*] your chance of becoming disabled is [*6 1/2*] times greater than your chance of dying.

We are able to offer a disability insurance plan that pays:

- ✔ [*70%*] of your present income up to [*$3,000*] per month
- ✔ Payments that are not reduced because of any other benefits you receive
- ✔ Your premiums are waived if you are totally disabled for [*60*] days
- ✔ A policy that is guaranteed renewable to age [*65*]

I will be calling you in a few days to obtain some basic information so that I can provide you with a no-obligation quote on protecting your income.

It costs nothing to listen, and it could mean an uninterrupted income flow.

Yours truly,

____

NOTE: *This mailer should be targeted at younger wage-earners.*

Individual Medical Insurance

[*Date*]

____
____
____

Dear ____________:

Health Insurance Is Expensive

But

There are alternatives.

- Higher deductibles
- Preferred provider plans
- Health maintenance plans
- And there is more

[*Call today and we will send you (a computer printout showing you) costs for alternative health care options.*]

Jeffrey Hopkins

398-2121

[*I will be calling you in a few days to obtain some basic information so that I can prepare a computer printout showing you costs for alternative health care options.*]

Yours truly,

____

NOTE: *Letters on health care coverage should be directed at individuals who are self-employed and thus unlikely to have group coverage.*

Hospitalization Insurance

[*Date*]

____
____
____

Dear __________:

We can now offer:

Affordable Hospitalization Insurance
at Group Rates
for the Self-Employed

- Quality benefits
- Discount price of a large group
- Flexible program choice to meet your needs

Call me at [*347-8011*]

for more information, or return the request form for a no-obligation quotation.

Yours truly,

____

Enclosure

Individual Medical Insurance HMOs and PPOs

[*Date*]

____
____
____

Dear __________:

Think You Can't Afford Medical Insurance?

Health insurance is attainable at an affordable cost with our unique

Managed Care Policy

Complete the enclosed information sheet and I will send you, without obligation, a rate quote that spells out what is or is not covered in clear understandable terms.

Interested? Then Don't Delay!

Yours truly,

____

Enclosure

NOTE: *The information sheet would be based on carrier guidelines.*

Catastrophic Health Insurance

[*Date*]

____
____
____

Dear __________:

What Is
Catastrophic Health Insurance?

It's a health insurance plan that is tailored to the needs of the [*small business owner*] [*professional*].

If you are like most [*small business owners*] [*professionals*], it is the worst-case scenario that really troubles you, a catastrophic illness where medical costs can mean financial ruin.

While an all-inclusive family health plan can be expected to cost between $5,000 and $9,000 per year, we can provide a health care plan tailored to your needs from [*Mutual of North Dakota*] for just about [*$150*] per month.

What's the catch? Well, there is one: a [*$5,000*] deductible [*per person*]. If you are the kind of person who can afford the first [*$5,000*] in health care costs each year, we can insure the [*$995,000*] in coverage up to [*$1,000,000*] per year [*per family member*].

The insurance carrier saves in avoiding the cost and administrative paperwork of dozens of small claims, and you get the protection you really want at a reasonable price.

[*I will be calling you in a few days to answer any questions you may have and to prepare a quote based on your specific needs.*]

Yours truly,

____

P.S. I can also quote you on a low-cost group rate for your employees based on various deductible amounts.

Medicare Supplemental Health Insurance

[*Date*]

____
____
____

Dear __________:

I know you will agree that:

Medicare Is Great!

Well, Almost!

What about the portion that Medicare doesn't pay? Drugs and copayments can wipe out the average retiree's savings in a matter of months.

There Is a Solution!

A low-cost Medicare supplemental insurance plan designed for your particular needs.

Interested?

I will call you in a few days to give you the particulars about a plan that can literally save your savings.

Yours truly,

____

Long-Term Care Coverage #1

[*Picture of beggar with tin cup and sign around neck*]

"Spouse in Nursing Home"

Could This Be You, [*Mr. or Mrs. Brown*]?

Know The Facts:

- Most supplemental insurance policies pay nothing for nursing home care.
- Medicare pays for only 100 days.
- Nursing home care can exceed $6,000 per month.
- Before you qualify for Medicaid, you will have to reduce yourself to pauper status. Of course with present nursing home costs, that may not take too long.

I will be calling you in the next few days to tell you about an affordable plan that will provide you with the protection you want. This could be one of the most important phone calls you will ever receive.

____

____

NOTE: *Mailing should be to people in more affluent retirement communities or from selective mailing lists of retirees.*

Long-Term Care Coverage #2

[*Date*]

____
____
____

Dear __________:

At Long Last
The Ultimate Long-Term Care Coverage

- Nursing home care
- No exclusion for Alzheimer's disease
- Benefits provided in hospital
- Benefits provided at home

Rates That Are Affordable

Interested? Then Call:
(628) 479-2121

Tom Riley Insurance
In the Town Plaza Center
2123 West Center

NOTE: *This letter could be used without the salutation as a flyer. It would be effective if left in nursing homes, retirement centers and doctors' offices.*

Chapter 6

Casualty Insurance Solicitation Letters

Auto Insurance—Low-Cost

[*Date*]

____
____
____

Dear ____________:

Who Has It All?

- Lowest-Cost Auto Insurance
- Monthly Rates

Teens—Seniors—Military—Problem Drivers
Canceled—Refused—Sports Cars—Motorcycles

We Handle Them All

Plus

Good-Driver Discounts

Call now for a free rate quote and you'll see who can give you more for less.

____

[*1-800-621-9843*]

Auto Insurance—Safe Driver

[*Date*]

____
____
____

Dear ____________:

All Drivers Are Not Equal!

At last there is a plan to reward experienced, safe drivers with a special low premium.

The cost? Well, it's so low you may not believe it, but it's backed by one of the most reputable insurance companies in America.

For a free, no-obligation opportunity to see how much you can actually save, complete the following form, using the coverage of your current policy as a guide. A prepaid mailer is included for your convenience.

Yours truly,

____

Enc: 1

Auto Insurance—Retiree

[*Date*]

____
____
____

Dear ____________:

Did you know

Retirees Are Low-Risk Drivers?

So Why Should You Pay the Same Rate as Bad Drivers?

Retirees:

- Drive fewer miles
- Have fewer accidents
- Are less likely to have their car stolen or vandalized in high-crime areas

I will call you in a few days to determine if you qualify for [*Mutual of Oxnard's*] [*Retirement Driver's Plan*]. I may be able to save you hundreds of dollars!

Yours truly,

____

Auto Insurance—High-Risk

[*Date*]

____
____
____

Dear ____________:

Do You Have a Problem with Automobile Insurance?

- DWI
- Too many traffic violations
- Under 21

Don't give up hope, we can cover just about anyone.
Call me toll-free today for a free rate quote.

[*Tom Brown*]
[*Brown's Insurance*]
[*1-800-340-3660*]

NOTE: *Consider using a postcard mailer to underaged drivers, as well as selective mailing lists that fall into the high-risk category.*

Auto Insurance—Deal with a Local Agent

[*Date*]

____
____
____

Dear ____________:

Homer Fink Saves $20

Homer Fink buys his auto insurance by mail order from Mutual of East Kalamazoo Insurance Company and has super savings. Homer is a pretty smart guy.

Of course, when Homer has a claim, he must fill out forms with no one to help him. Homer doesn't even mind that when he has a problem he must call long distance and talk to a machine. Eventually the claims do get paid—well, most of them. After all, the $20 makes it all worthwhile. Why, that amounts to $1.66 each and every month, and that's about five cents per day.

But perhaps you would prefer to work with a real person, not a machine. A local person who understands your needs, who will recommend changes in coverages when needed, who will answer your questions and who will be there for you when you need [*him*] [*her*]. I hope so.

I will be calling you in the next few days to introduce myself, [*Jeff Higgins*] [*Kathy Gale*], offering full family insurance protection with service.

Yours truly,

____

Auto/Homeowner Insurance—Deal with a Local Agent

[*Date*]

____
____
____

Dear ____________:

Do You Buy Automobile or Homeowner Insurance
Through the Mail?

If so, I hope you never have to try to collect a claim.

I am a real person, not a post office box or a number that's always busy. You can get to know me face to face. I'm here when you have problems, and sooner or later we all do have them.

I can give you coverage tailored to your own needs at prices you didn't think were possible from a full-service agent.

I will call you in a few days to show you the advantages of dealing with a real person.

Yours truly,

____

Motorcycle Insurance

[*Date*]

____
____
____

Dear ____________:

I specialize in:

Motorcycle Insurance

- Liability Coverage
- Collision
- Medical Pay
- Comprehensive [*Fire/ Theft/ Vandalism*]
- Uninsured Motorist

Lowest Rates
[*Monthly or Semiannual Premiums*]
Call Today for a Free Rate Quote
1-800-821-3764
[*Jeffrey Higgins*]

NOTE: *As an alternative, the above mailer can be a heavier-stock paper, with the bottom portion as a tear-off postcard with the necessary information for a quote.*

By offering a product aimed at a specialized interest group, you will be regarded as a specialist for that group. You will also be able to network effectively within the group for other coverage. Other variations are:

Sports car insurance
Truck insurance
RV insurance
Snowmobile insurance
Water ski insurance
ATV insurance

Homeowner Insurance—New Purchaser

[*Date*]

____

____

____

Dear ___________:

Welcome to our neighborhood.

The records of the [*Charlotte Board of Realtors®*] indicate that you will shortly be the new owner of a lovely home at [*1127 Chippendale Road*]. I have prepared a computer printout of a homeowner insurance package based on your new home purchase. Note that all coverages are plainly set forth, as well as the annual premium (which can be paid in semiannual payments). I would aid you at closing time by supplying your lender with information on insurance coverage upon your request.

I will call you in a few days to discuss the coverage I have recommended. Whether or not you decide to retain me as your agent, I would like to welcome you to our neighborhood. If there is any way I can help you in your move, please don't hesitate to let me know.

Sincerely,

____

NOTE: *Membership in a local real estate multiple listing service might be necessary for you to obtain access to sale information, and even then you might not obtain the buyer's name and address. You might have to request this information from the listing or selling real estate agent. You can readily see where networking with real estate agents could be a source of business. If you were recommended by the selling agent, the first sentence should read, "[Anne Jeffries of Long Point Realty] suggested I contact you about your recent house purchase at [__________________]."*

Expansion of Homeowner Coverage

[*Date*]

____
____
____

Dear ____________:

What if...

[*Picture of burglar running from home with a bag of loot and a fur coat*]

Did you know most homeowner policies have limits as low as $500 for loss of

- Jewelry
- Silver
- Furs
- Art objects
- Collections (stamps, coins, guns, etc.)

I will be calling in a few days to arrange to provide you with an audit of your current insurance protection. This no-cost, no-obligation audit will inform you (in writing) of areas of financial exposure and the costs of obtaining necessary coverage if desired.

Sincerely,

____

Homeowner–Auto Combined Policy

[*Date*]

____
____
____

Dear __________:

If you are like most people, you have a homeowner insurance policy and a separate automobile policy. Now it's possible to combine them with a single policy.

- It makes sense.
- It saves dollars.

Check your coverage and what you pay on both of these policies. You will be amazed at how much you are now paying. I will be calling you in a few days to give you a free quote on a combination policy based upon your current coverage.

Yours truly,

____

Earthquake Insurance

[*Date*]

____
____
____

Dear ____________:

"The Big One!"

It could happen, and the experts say it will. An earthquake could leave you with a pile of rubble and a mortgage obligation as well.

Earthquake coverage provides financial protection and, most importantly, peace of mind.

I will be calling you in a few days to show you how little this protection actually costs.

Yours truly,

____

NOTE: *This letter is aimed at owners living in close proximity to geological fault lines.*

Flood Insurance

[*Date*]

____
____
____

Dear ____________:

Flood!

No, I don't know what the weather will be, but it has sure been strange the last few years. We are experiencing more record rains every year, and news broadcasts show homes being inundated by flood waters.

Sure you have homeowner's insurance, but homeowner policies exclude flood loss. That's right, your home and possessions can be ruined and your insurance carrier won't give you one dime—that is, unless you carry flood insurance.

I will be calling you in a few days to talk with you about how little it actually costs to gain this important protection for your home and possessions.

Yours truly,

____

Renter's Insurance

[*Date*]

____
____
____

Dear __________:

Renters Don't Need Insurance

Well, that's what most renters think. I know they think this way, because very few renters insure their belongings.

On the other hand, for weeks after every disaster, the late news features hundreds of former renters living in tent cities or in high school gymnasiums. They have no place to live, no belongings and no insurance.

As a renter you can obtain a [*Renter's Protection Policy*] very similar to a property owner's plan, but at much lower cost. It can cover:

- Your household goods [*at replacement value*] from losses due to fire, storm, [*flood*] [*and other disasters*]. This includes furniture, clothing [*and even cameras, guns and some jewelry*].
- Theft and vandalism protection for your possessions.
- [*Cost of living expense caused by destruction of property.*]
- [*Liability protection from claims of others who are injured by your acts or the acts of family members.*]
- [*Medical pay for injuries to guests.*]

I will be calling you in just a few days to obtain some basic information in order to provide a no-obligation quote on our [*Tenant Protection Plan*]. I think you will be pleasantly surprised to find out how inexpensive protection really is.

Yours truly,

____

NOTE: *You might want to include an insurance company brochure on Renter's Insurance. Keep in mind, this policy can be an entry for other coverage in the future.*

Landlord Policy

[*Date*]

____
____
____

Dear ___________:

At last there is protection just for you.

Landlord's Insurance

- Your building is covered.
- [*Any additional 1–4-unit structure you purchase during the term of the policy is covered for ___________ days.*]
- Your personal property is covered.
- [*We protect you against rent loss due to a covered loss.*]
- We even cover your landscaping.

Interested in just one policy that is designed to meet all your needs? I will be calling you in a few days to tell you more about this comprehensive coverage including its lower than expected cost and to answer any questions you might have.

Yours truly,

____

Umbrella Policy #1

[*Date*]

____
____
____

Dear ____________:

What's an Umbrella?

An umbrella is an insurance policy that takes over where your other insurance policies leave off. It provides a high personal liability limit in addition to your regular insurance coverage. As an example, if you carry a $500,000 limit on your automobile insurance, a $1,000,000 umbrella would effectively raise your coverage to $1,500,000. In these days of million-dollar-plus legal judgments, this coverage makes good financial sense.

The Good Part

The cost for a $1,000,000 umbrella is likely to be around 50¢ a day. [*Call me today for an exact quote*] [*I will be calling you in a few days to give you an exact quote*]. I will need to know your current limits of liability on both your homeowner's and automobile policies.

Yours truly,

____

[*John Henry Insurance*]

[*1-800-673-9240*]

Umbrella Policy #2

[*Date*]

____

____

____

Dear ____________:

Are You Half Naked?

With the jury verdicts we are seeing in the papers, it seems that no insurance is enough. It wasn't many years ago that most people only carried $25,000 limits as to total liability on auto and homeowner policies. Slowly the limits rose to $100,000, $300,000 and even $1,000,000. A million dollars, while a lot of money, may not be enough. A one-and-one-half million dollar judgment from an accident, even with a million in coverage, leaves you just one-half million dollars short.

There is an answer: a low-cost [*$1,000,000*] umbrella policy that is only [*$145*] per year if your present auto and homeowner's policies have [*$1,000,000*] limits. Does [*$145*] seem like a sensible investment for another [*$1,000,000*] of coverage?

I will be calling you in the next few days to answer any questions you might have about umbrella liability protection.

Sincerely,

____

Waterbed Insurance

ATTENTION! LANDLORDS!

A tenant's leaky waterbed can mean

$ THOUSANDS $

in serious property damage.

Have your tenant protect you with

Waterbed Insurance

For only [*$28 per year*], a tenant can protect you for leakage damage up to:

$25,000
[*Carson Insurance*]
[*256 West Main*]
[*(714) 328-7676*]

[*Enc: Tenant waterbed insurance application cards.*]

NOTE: *This letter can be sent to owners and managers of apartments as well as to property management firms. A low-cost tenant waterbed insurance policy is a first step toward greater coverage for the tenant.*

Collector's Coverage

[*Date*]

____
____
____

Dear ____________:

How's your [*stamp*] collection?

Is your collection adequately protected against:

- Fire
- Flood
- Vandalism
- Theft

The bad news is that most homeowner policies have relatively low limits for loss for a collection such as yours.

The good news is that it likely costs less than you think to obtain coverage for your valuable collection.

[*For specific details call me at (717-347-8241).*]

[*I will be calling you in a few days to get some basic information so that I can prepare a no-obligation quote based on your specific needs.*]

Sincerely,

____

NOTE: *This letter could be tailored for baseball card collections, antiques, guns, etc. Use of a specialized mailing list of collectors will allow you to pinpoint a group.*

The letter could also be used as a flyer to be given out at collector shows.

Boat, Snowmobile, Jet Ski Insurance

[*Date*]

____
____
____

Dear _____________:

We can provide you with

[*Boat*] Insurance

Up to [*$10,000*] Coverage

✓ Fire

✓ Theft

✓ Vandalism

Only [*$8.40*] Per Month

Liability Coverage Also Available

Call Now for Lowest Rates

____

[*(717) 374-8238*]

NOTE: *The letter could be tailored for jet skis, snowmobiles, etc. It could also be used as a flyer and left where boats are sold, stored and repaired.*

Home Computer Insurance

[*Date*]

____
____
____

Dear __________:

Is Your Memory Protected?

Most home computers are only protected against fire or theft damage.

What if:

- You drop your printer?
- Your dog chews up your software?
- Your son's hockey puck is incompatible with your color monitor?

We offer complete protection.

- All risk (not specifically excluded)
- Basic unit, peripherals, memory expanders, cartridges, disks and commercially available software
- Full replacement cost (no deductible or depreciation)
- Business use of home system will not void the coverage
- You decide on how much coverage you should have

The cost? Just pennies a day! Just fill out the enclosed postcard indicating how much coverage you want for a free, no-obligation quote.

____

Yes! Send me a no-cost, no-obligation quote on protection for my home computer system.

Name: ____________________ Telephone: ______________

Address: ____

Dollar value of coverage desired: $ ________________

Floater Policy

[*Date*]

____
____
____

Dear ____________:

What's a Floater?

It's an insurance policy that provides coverage for valuables normally not fully protected by homeowner policies, such as:

- ✓ Furs
- ✓ Jewelry
- ✓ Paintings
- ✓ Antiques
- ✓ Computers

While we can't replace a lost objet d'art, we can see that you get full value should you suffer a loss.

Call me today at [*321-4171*] for a no-obligation rate quote. It costs far less than you imagined to have the coverage you need.

Yours truly,

____

Worker's Compensation—Household Help

Do You Have Full-Time or Part-Time Help?

What happens if:

- Your cleaning lady is injured in your home
- The gardener has an accident with the mower
- The baby-sitter gets food poisoning

Most homeowners don't realize they could be liable for employee on-the-job injuries, and that they are exposing themselves to financial dangers that homeowner's policies seldom cover. If you employ someone in your home, you need Worker's Compensation Coverage or you will place your assets at risk.

[*If you have part-time or full-time help, call me to find out how easy and inexpensive it is to protect yourself. It could be the most important phone call of your life.*]

[*I will call you in a few days to obtain some basic information so that I can prepare a quote based on your specific needs.*]

Yours truly,

____

[*Your Worker's Compensation Specialist*]

NOTE: *This letter should target more affluent areas.*

Chapter

7

Solicitation Letters for Other Financial Products and Services

Financial Planning Solicitation #1

[*Date*]

____

____

____

Dear ____________:

I WON'T TRY TO SELL YOU INSURANCE

What I would like to do is to talk to you about total financial planning that includes maximizing your spendable income, reducing income tax, providing adequate resources for retirement needs, providing family protection, reducing or eliminating estate taxes and eliminating probate costs. Depending upon your circumstances, my recommendations may or may not include an insurance plan. However, any decision must be yours.

I will call you in the next few days to set up an appointment to determine your specific needs and how they can best be met.

Sincerely,

____

Financial Planning Solicitation #2

[*Date*]

____
____
____

Dear ____________:

Ask yourself:

What Can Financial Planning Do for Me?

How About:

- Increased Spendable Income
- Increased Retirement Income
- Lower or No Estate Taxes
- Elimination of Probate Costs
- Family Protection

Interested?
Call me for a no-cost, no-obligation consultation.

Yours truly,

____

Financial Planning Solicitation #3

[*Date*]

____
____
____

Dear ____________:

Who Needs Financial Planning?

Perhaps you do. You don't have to be a millionaire to benefit from financial planning. Planning your financial future now could:

- ✓ Increase your retirement income.
- ✓ Reduce and, in most cases, eliminate the cost and delay of probate.
- ✓ Simplify the paperwork burden for your heirs.
- ✓ Provide for the immediate cash needs of your survivors.
- ✓ Save many thousands of dollars in estate taxes.

Think about it—is this what you want? I will call you in the next few days to arrange a short, no-cost, no-obligation meeting where I can learn about your specific needs and explain our services.

Sincerely,

____

Financial Planning Solicitation #4

[*Date*]

____
____
____

Dear __________:

Can You Live on $_________/Month?

Well, you might have to live on even less, because that's the current *maximum* Social Security benefit, and most people get far less.

Does an additional $1,000 per month interest you? Or how about $2,000 or even more? This is not pie-in-the-sky talk; it's the dollars and sense of financial planning starting *NOW*!

I will be calling you in a few days to discover your particular financial needs and to prepare, at no cost or obligation to you, a plan to achieve these needs.

Yours truly,

____

Financial Planning Solicitation #5

[*Date*]

____
____
____

Dear ____________:

Don't Take My Word for It!

My Clients Can Prove It!

They can prove that I can prepare a plan to cut federal (and state) tax liability and insure retirement income.

I have enclosed statements by local residents whom I have worked with to back up my claim.

I will be calling you in a few days to discuss how I can help to meet your financial needs.

Yours truly,

____

Enclosures

Financial Planning Solicitation #6

[*Date*]

____
____
____

Dear __________:

[*$1,000,000*] in Cash!

No, I'm not selling lottery tickets. What I can offer you is an estate plan that can provide that amount on your retirement plus offer tax savings that will make the IRS very unhappy.

Best of all, this is no gamble. I can tailor a program for you that will meet the goals that you set.

Want To Know More?

I will call you in the next few days to obtain some basic information so that I can prepare a no-obligation proposal for your retirement plan at a cost that will be far less than you imagined.

Yours truly,

____

Financial Planning Solicitation #7

[*Date*]

____
____
____

Dear ____________:

[One-dollar bill attached to letter]

Enclosed is a $1 bill. I want to stop you from needlessly giving thousands of these bills to the IRS.

Not only can I help you in keeping more of your earned income in your pocket; I can also help you avoid a costly probate and totally eliminate or greatly reduce taxes on your estate.

I will be calling you in a few days to tell you how professional financial planning can meet your needs.

Yours truly,

____

NOTE: *This letter is effective because recipients feel obligated to listen to what you have to say. You also obtained their interest with something very close to their hearts.*

Financial Planning—New Parent

[*Date*]

____
____
____

Dear ____________:

IT WILL COST YOU $100,000

That's what a four-year college degree is going to cost for your [*son John*] [*daughter Mary*], and that's for a state college based on present costs and estimated future increases.

I CAN GET IT FOR YOU

I can tailor a plan for you and your child's needs to provide you with the college funds when they are needed at a present monthly cost that is far less than you imagined.

WANT TO KNOW MORE?

I will call you in a few days to obtain some basic information so that I can provide you with a no-obligation proposal tailored to your needs.

Yours truly,

____

Coupon—Retirement Analysis

Free Offer!

Issued to: Jane Smith
1711 West Sycamore
Clifton Heights, VA 92743

This coupon is good for one FREE (computer-generated) retirement analysis which will tell you what income you can expect to be receiving in terms of real dollars adjusted for anticipated inflation upon your retirement.

To validate this offer, complete the enclosed data sheet and return to:

The Jones Agency
3721 Maple Street
Clifton Heights, VA 92743

(Postage-free return envelope enclosed)

NOTE: *This coupon could be used as an enclosure with other mailings to prospective clients as well as present clients.*

Attachment to Retirement Planning Coupon

Confidential Retirement Information

[Jane Smith
1711 West Sycamore
Clifton Heights, VA 92743]

Date of Birth [ ]

Anticipated Retirement Date: [ ]

Do you have a company retirement plan? ________.
If yes, approximate percentage of income you will receive [or dollar amount]: ________.
Current gross monthly income: $________.
Do you have a private retirement fund? ________. If yes, the monthly benefits you will receive on date of retirement: $________.
How many years will you have worked under Social Security at the time of your retirement? ________.
Current amount of savings in cash, stocks, bonds, certificates of deposit, etc.? $________.
The amount of additional savings that you hope to accumulate by your retirement date: $________.
Amount of any other monthly income that you anticipate receiving after retirement date: $________.
Number of children: ________.
Ages of children: ________.
Do you have any parent or in-law who might require some financial support from you? ________.
If you plan to retire prior to age 65, will your employer's plan continue to pay your health insurance premiums? ________.

Retirement Planning Solicitation #1

[*Date*]

____
____
____

Dear ____________:

Do You Need an Individual Retirement Plan?

In today's world with corporate layoffs at every level and underfunded employee retirement plans, if you want a guaranteed retirement program, it had better be your own.

You don't have to start from scratch, because I have a number of plans that can be tailored to your needs. Whether it is having the money to buy a retirement home, paying for your children's college education or just maintaining or upgrading the quality of your life, I can show you how to meet those needs.

I will be calling in a few days to arrange an appointment so that we can evaluate your needs. I will then prepare a plan for your consideration. The rest is up to you.

I look forward to meeting with you. I am sure you will agree that your future is worth a few minutes of your time.

Sincerely,

____

Retirement Planning Solicitation #2

[*Date*]

____
____
____

Dear ____________:

Have You Started Your Retirement Planning?
Where's Your 33%?

According to the U.S. Department of Health and Human Services, 33% of your income during retirement will come from personal savings and investments, and that's if you are satisfied being average.

Retirement need not be a time of reduced expectations and penny pinching. I can show you where that 33% and a lot more will come from.

I'll be calling you within a few days about a unique investment plan for living that I feel certain will interest you.

Yours truly,

____

Retirement Plan Maximization

[*Date*]

____
____
____

Dear ____________:

Want To Be Able To Maximize Your Pension?

- $100s more of spendable income each month
- Life benefits plus money for your estate
- Safety
- Benefits that are free of income taxation

Want to know more about our ["*Pension Max*"] plan? I will be calling you in a few days with more details about a simple plan to increase the yield of your current retirement plan.

____

NOTE: *Pensioner chooses single-life option under company retirement plan for highest yield and uses part of the money gained to buy an insurance policy on his or her life with spouse as beneficiary. If pensioner dies, spouse receives a lump sum payment. Death benefits are free of income tax. Compare this to the normal joint and survivor annuity with far lower payments that end when the last survivor dies, leaving nothing for the estate.*

Retirement Plan Rollover

[*Date*]

____
____
____

Dear ____________:

Is Your Retirement Plan Giving You
[*8%*] Interest?

The Employee Retirement Income Security Act of 1974 (ERISA) permits the tax-free transfer of retirement savings from one plan to another. It's called a tax-free rollover.

I will call you in a few days to discuss your present retirement plan and to show you the advantages of a rollover into a higher-yield program. After all, it's your money and your future.

Yours truly,

____

IRA

[*Date*]

____
____
____

Dear ____________:

What Is an IRA?

It is a government-authorized individual retirement account that allows a taxpayer to avoid taxes on part of his or her income by putting funds into the account before taxes are considered. Best of all, the earnings are also exempt from taxes until the money is taken out after retirement.

I will be calling you in a few days to ascertain if you are eligible for an IRA or any other tax-saving plan currently authorized by the IRS.

Yours truly,

____

NOTE: *For those not eligible for an IRA, or other tax shelter annuity, consider traditional whole life coverage.*

TSA

[*Date*]

____
____
____

Dear __________:

Want a Tax Break?

As an employee of a [*nonprofit educational institution*] you are eligible under Internal Revenue Code Sections 403(b) and 501(c) for a Tax-Sheltered Annuity (TSA). Let me tell you what a TSA can mean for you:

✓ Your contributions are excluded from your gross income. (No tax is paid on earnings invested in your TSA.)

✓ Earnings accumulate free from income taxation.

✓ You can use your TSA to significantly supplement your retirement plans.

I will be calling you in a few days to tell you more about the significant tax breaks and the variety of programs available using a TSA.

Yours truly,

____

NOTE: *Eligible employers for a tax-deferred annuity [TSA] include:*

✓ *Public and private elementary and secondary schools as well as public and private universities*

✓ *Zoos, museums, research and scientific foundations*

✓ *Private hospitals and medical schools*

✓ *Churches and religious organizations*

Estate Tax/Life Insurance

[*Date*]

____

____

____

Dear ____________:

That portion of your estate over $600,000 will be taxed under Federal Estate Tax guidelines.

This tax can mean that over 50 percent of your estate will be lost to your heirs.

By coordinating a life insurance product into your estate plan, you can provide an undiminished estate for your heirs. Are you interested?

I will be calling you in a few days to tell you more about how you can avoid losing a large part of your estate to taxation.

Yours truly,

____

NOTE: *This letter would be directed to affluent prospects.*

College Fundraising Through Estate Planning

[*Date*]

____
____
____

Dear ____________:

Can you use thousands of dollars, hundreds of thousands or even millions for:

- ✓ Scholarship funds
- ✓ New buildings
- ✓ Endowed chairs
- ✓ Operating expenses

I believe I can help you achieve your goals by making it easier for donors to make substantial gifts to you. I'm talking about programs that offer signficant benefits to the donor during his or her life. While it may be more blessed to give than to receive, it nevertheless makes sense to make being blessed as easy as possible.

I will be calling in a few days to set up an appointment to show you what I have in mind.

Sincerely,

____

NOTE: *This letter could go to college presidents, alumni associations and booster clubs. This letter could be used for split life (term and annuity), in which the donor keeps the insurance portion and gives the annuity to the school with the annuity payments tax-deductible. With such a program, your leads would come from the school.*

Charity Fundraising Through Estate Planning

[*Date*]

____
____
____

Dear ____________:

As you realize, large donors are a fiscal necessity to the growth of a [*charitable organization*] [*church*].

While I am not able to write that one check that will meet all of your financial needs, I believe I can be of help to you in securing large donors. I propose to work with you and potential donors to tailor both lifetime and estate gifts in order to maximize the tax benefits to the donor and at the same time improve the financial security of [*name of organization*]. Because potential large donors are subjected to many requests upon their resources, what I propose is to give your [*organization*] [*church*] a competitive advantage.

I will be calling in the next few days to arrange to meet with [*you*] [*you and your board of directors*] to map out a plan to secure large gifts for your [*organization*] [*church*].

Sincerely,

____

NOTE: *See note on previous letter.*

Chapter 8

Business Insurance Solicitation Letters

Business Audit Solicitation

[*Date*]

____
____
____

Dear __________:

A Child with a Rock

could cause thousands of dollars in plate glass window loss. You might be lucky and the merchandise *may* not be taken from the window. In the real world, however, your entire store could be looted and vandalized, if not set ablaze. Where once you had stock and fixtures, you could be left with rubble. Even if you had the funds to rebuild, the delays in construction and getting permits could not only erode what savings are left, but also cause you to lose your key employees and clientele. This explains why so few businesses ever fully recover from a calamity.

Now the above is just one of dozens of possible scenarios that can spell ruin for an otherwise successful business.

I will be calling you in the next few days to arrange a meeting. The purpose: to provide you with a written audit of your present coverage as well as exposure to loss. I will also provide you with costs to fill exposure areas so you can intelligently make your business insurance decisions.

Yours truly,

____

Business Insurance (General)

[Date]

____
____
____

Dear ____________:

Did you know that there is an insurance program tailored for [*hardware store owners*] [*small business owners*] such as you that includes:

- Protection of your inventory from loss by [*fire, flood, theft or vandalism*];
- Protection from robbery or burglary;
- Protection of your fixtures from fire, flood or vandalism; and
- Inclusion of high-limit liability coverage.

In addition, we can add:

- Plate glass protection;
- Business interruption coverage;
- Protection of your vehicles;
- Worker's compensation coverage;
- And even employee and owner benefit packages.

I will be calling you in a few days to show you what it means in dollars and sense to obtain all of your business protection from a single small business protection specialist.

Yours truly,

____

Business Coverage (Specific Type of Business)

[*Date*]

____

____

____

Dear ____________:

As [*a wholesaler*] [*an appliance dealer*] [*a beauty shop operator*], you know your business and its needs.

Now you can have an insurance program designed to meet the specific needs of [*a wholesaler*] [*an appliance dealer*] [*a beauty shop operator*].

I will be calling you in a few days to obtain some basic information so that I can prepare a no-obligation quote on the coverage you want and need.

It costs nothing to listen and compare. It could save your business.

Yours truly,

____

Partnership Insurance

[*Date*]

____
____
____

Dear ____________:

What If Your Partner Died?

Your choices would be simple:

1. *Pay off your partner's heirs.*
   Even if you could raise the cash necessary to pay off the heirs and retain operating capital, it would result in business debt and debt service costs that could result in failure of what otherwise was a very successful business.
2. *Liquidate the business.*
   Give up all you have worked for at what will likely be a bargain-basement price.

There Is a Third Choice

3. *Insurance.*
   By the creative use of insurance, you can invest in the continuity of your business and pay off heirs while actually increasing business assets.

I will be calling you in a few days to tell you more about how this third choice can work for you. Best of all, you will see that it really doesn't cost you anything.

Yours truly,

____

NOTE: *By the use of a whole life product, the partnership is actually making an investment, not paying an operational cost.*

Partnership—Disability Buyout

[*Date*]

____

____

____

Dear ____________:

What If Your Partner Is Disabled?

No matter what the cause, it is going to mean the loss of the use of a valuable asset that will have to be replaced with salaried employees. Plus, your partner would still be entitled to his or her share of profits, benefits and possibly even salary.

Don't Want to Worry about It?

There is a way. It is a disability buyout plan that costs less than you would imagine and will meet the needs of all of the partners as well as ensure the continuity of the partnership.

I will be calling you in a few days to tell you more about this important protection.

Yours truly,

____

Close Corporations—Buyout Insurance

[*Date*]

____
____
____

Dear ____________:

Certainly close corporations are great. They have tax and liability advantages, but:

What If a Shareholder Dies?

There are several possible scenarios, including:

1. Taking someone into the business who is not qualified or motivated
2. Having to deal with dissident shareholders
3. Raising the cash to pay off shareholders who likely have a distorted view of the corporation value

There Is a Solution

It is simple and it costs far less than you imagine.

I will be calling you in a few days to obtain some basic information so that I can prepare a no-obligation proposal that will meet the best interest of both you and your corporation.

Yours truly,

____

Close Corporation—Disability Buyout

[*Date*]

____
____
____

Dear ____________:

What If a Shareholder Is Disabled?

No matter what the cause, it is going to mean the loss of a key principal in your business who will likely have to be replaced by salaried employees.

Plus, the disabled shareholder will still be entitled to share in the dividends and likely in the benefits as well.

There Is a Solution

With a disability shareholder buyout plan you can meet both the shareholder's and corporate needs. Best of all, it costs far less than you would imagine.

I will be calling you in a few days to tell you more about this important protection.

Yours truly,

____

Inland Marine Protection

[*Date*]

____
____
____

Dear ____________:

You don't need to own a boat to be concerned about

Inland Marine Protection

Inland Marine Protection is business insurance covering:

- ✓ Accounts receivable (due to destruction of records)
- ✓ Valuable papers and records
- ✓ Goods in transit
- ✓ Property of others in your possession
- ✓ Tools and equipment, and a great deal more

I will be calling you in a few days to arrange, at no cost or obligation, a review of your coverage. If I find any leaks, I will recommend coverage to keep you afloat.

Yours truly,

____

Business Interruption Insurance

[*Date*]

____
____
____

Dear ___________:

Close Your Business for Six Months

Heaven forbid, but it could happen. A fire or other disaster could easily mean being closed down for six months or even longer. You could easily expect:

- 1 month to settle with your insurance company.
- 5 months or more to rebuild or find another location, design premises, obtain permits, construction work, decorating, new fixtures, supplies, hiring and training new personnel, etc.

A six-month closing would mean:

- Loss of Cash Flow: You would likely have to use a significant portion of your insurance proceeds (or savings) for your own living expenses.
- Payment of Rent and other expenses for a new location while the premises are being prepared.
- Loss of Key People: Unless you can pay your key people while you are closed, you will lose them. This means new hires and training them. Even then it could be many months or years before the present proficiency is obtained.
- Loss of Clientele: Your customers will have gone elsewhere while you were closed. It could take years to recover from a six-month closure.

And some businesses take a year or more to reopen. What would that cost?

You can readily see why many profitable businesses have had difficulty recovering from disasters, even when they had insurance coverage for their stock, inventory and building.

I don't mean to give you a sleepless night of worry. I simply want to point out that there could be a very serious problem, but there is also a solution. I will be calling you in a few days to set up an appointment to discuss your needs and to explain how a unique business interruption policy offered by [*Pennsylvania Insurance Group*] can fit those needs.

Sincerely,

____

NOTE: *A long letter will be read in its entirety if you can grab the reader's attention in the first paragraph.*

Disability Overhead Expense

[*Date*]

____
____
____

Dear ____________:

What Will Happen to Your [*Business*] [*Practice*]
If You Become Disabled?

Your [*office*] [*business*] expenses will still be there. You can't shut down, as this will mean the loss of [*customers*] [*clients*] [*patients*] as well as your key personnel. [*Once a business has closed its doors, it seldom is able to recover.*]

Your personal disability insurance only protects your personal income. If you want your business to be protected, you need

Disability Overhead Expense Coverage

The good news is that:

1. The cost is a fully deductible business expense;
2. It likely costs far less than you imagine.

I will be calling you in a few days to obtain some basic information in order to provide you with a no-obligation quotation for coverage that meets your needs.

Yours truly,

____

Keyperson Insurance

[*Date*]

____
____
____

Dear __________:

Death of Employee = Business Loss

Many businesses have gone under because of the loss of income and/or knowledge occasioned by an employee's death.

If you have an essential employee, you can insure against this risk with

KEYPERSON INSURANCE

This is a low-cost term policy of life insurance that pays the employer the face amount of the policy upon the death of the key employee.

NOTE: You can use this coverage as an employee retention benefit by providing that the proceeds upon death be split between the employee's named beneficiaries and you, the employer.

I will be calling you within the next few days to determine if Keyperson Insurance can play a role in insuring your business prosperity.

Yours truly,

____

Disability Coverage—Key Employee

[*Date*]

____
____
____

Dear ____________:

What If a Key Employee Becomes Disabled? Do You Continue His or Her Paycheck?

If you do, you will certainly help employee morale and the retention of other key employees, but you could be letting yourself in for a shock.

If you are not contractually obligated to pay the employee, continued payments could be regarded by the IRS as gifts to the employee, which would mean you would be taxed on the payments as if you never made them.

There Is a Solution

A low-cost tax-deductible disability income protection plan for key employees.

I will be calling you in the next few days to obtain some basic information so that I can prepare a no-obligation proposal on providing this very important employee benefit. Incidentally, the cost could be shared by you and your employee.

Yours truly,

____

Professional Malpractice or Business Liability

[*Date*]

____
____
____

Dear ____________:

The More You Have

the more likely some former [*patient*] [*client*] [*customer*] is going to sue you. It makes no difference that your judgment was proper and your actions were professionally sound, the thought of getting their hands into your pockets can change a person's perception of what you said or did.

You can find yourself before a jury including people who may be envious of your success and sympathize with what will appear to be a pathetic plaintiff. Even if you win, the monetary and emotional costs can be staggering.

That is the risk of [*your chosen profession*] [*being in business*] in today's environment. My profession, on the other hand, is to evaluate these risks and to provide a plan to meet your needs at a sensible cost. I will be calling you in a few days to arrange a short meeting. A few minutes of your time can save years of aggravation as well as what I believe will be a significant cash savings.

Sincerely,

____

NOTE: *This letter could be sent to doctors, attorneys, accountants, small business owners, etc.*

Malpractice Insurance

[*Date*]

____
____
____

Dear ____________:

A Whoops! Or No Whoops!

It really doesn't matter, because a disgruntled [*client*] [*patient*] can always sue. A malpractice suit is an assault on your professional reputation as well as your wallet.

I represent [*Continental United*] [*a number of carriers*] and specialize in meeting the needs of professionals like yourself.

Right now I can't promise anything, but I may be able to:

- ✓ Save you money
- ✓ Provide increased malpractice coverage
- ✓ Provide you with greater peace of mind

I will be calling you in the next few days to get some basic information so that I can prepare a no-obligation quote. I think you will be interested in what I can do for you.

Yours truly,

____

Fidelity Bonds

[*Date*]

____
____
____

Dear ____________:

Did you hear about

The Trusted Bookkeeper

who walked away with the company's profits?

It Could Happen To You!

People you don't trust are not the people who are likely to take your money or goods. You wouldn't give them the opportunity to do so.

It is people you have absolute trust in, people you feel love and respect you, who are the embezzlers. These are the only people who handle cash, checks and billings in such a manner that theft becomes possible.

What Can You Do?

There is a simple answer. It costs far less than you think to obtain fidelity bonding for these key employees and let your trust rest easily.

I will be calling you in a few days to tell you more about this essential protection.

Yours truly,

____

Director's Liability

[*Date*]

____
____
____

Dear ____________:

It's Great To Be a Director!
Or Is It?

Do you realize that directors of [*condominium associations*] [*corporations*] can be held personally liable for their actions as directors, even though they thought their actions were in the best interests of the [*members*] [*stockholders*]?

Does your [*association*] [*corporation*] offer you adequate protection? With multimillion-dollar judgments almost an everyday occurrence, you should give thought to greater protection.

Call me for a free quote on a [*$10,000,000*] Director Liability policy for your [*association*] [*corporation*]. It could be the most important phone call of your life.

Yours truly,

____

Company Retirement Program

[*Date*]

____
____
____

Dear ____________:

It's Here at Last!

A Retirement Program for Small Business That Makes Sense.

- Safety
- High yield
- Personal choice in a variety of programs and benefits
- Tax benefits

And best of all, it ensures the retention of key employees.

I will call in the next few days to set up an appointment to show you how I can tailor a plan to meet the needs of you, your company and your employees. A few minutes of your time could affect your future in a very positive way.

Sincerely,

____

Employee Benefit Package

[*Date*]

____
____
____

Dear ____________:

As an employer you want:

Loyal Employees

who are not going to jump to another job offering a few dollars more.

I can help your quality employee retention with a unique

Supermarket of Benefits

Let your employees pick the benefits they want, such as:

- ✓ *Medical and dental (with a choice of deductibles)*
- ✓ *Extended care protection*
- ✓ *Accidental death or disability*
- ✓ *Retirement annuities (fixed or variable fund investments)*
- ✓ *Term life protection*

I will be calling you in a few days to tell you how to increase the effectiveness of your employee benefit dollar.

Yours truly,

____

Keogh Plan

[*Date*]

____
____
____

Dear ___________:

Let Me Tell You about a

Keogh Plan

Basically you may be eligible to invest 25 percent of your earned income, up to $30,000, in a retirement plan without having to pay taxes on the amount invested or on the earnings until you take the money out after retirement.

The IRS doesn't do very much for small business owners, but the Keogh Plan is an exception. Talk to your accountant. You will learn that the Keogh Plan is an opportunity that will mean more dollars for you on retirement.

I will call you in a few days to find out about your specific needs so that I can propose a Keogh Plan that will best meet those needs.

Yours truly,

____

Worker's Compensation Insurance

[*Date*]

____
____
____

Dear ____________:

Worker's Compensation Claims Are Rising!
So Are Premiums

Of course worker's compensation coverage is mandatory, but all coverage is not the same. We have a program designed for [*steel fabricators, the trucking industry, contractors*] that provides:

- On-the-job inspections
- Help in developing safety programs
- Reduction in job time loss
- Reduction in accidents
- [*Lower premium*] [*Premium discounts*]
- Efficient claim settlement

I will be calling you in a few days to obtain some basic information so that I can prepare a no-obligation quote. A few minutes of your time could mean significant direct and indirect savings.

Yours truly,

____

Nonemployee Group Coverage

[*Date*]

____

____

____

Dear ____________:

Are You a Group?

Did you realize the [*Order of Chipmunks*] qualifies as a group for insurance purposes?

You could offer your members low-cost:

- Health insurance benefits
- Medicare supplemental coverage
- Accidental death insurance
- Term life insurance
- Disability insurance
- Auto insurance
- Homeowner protection, and more

I will call you in a few days to set up an appointment to discuss the benefits you can offer to your members.

Yours truly,

____

NOTE: *This letter could be sent to local clubs or trade groups as well as national organizations headquartered in your area.*

Chapter 9

Client Letters

Letter after Meeting (Sale or No-Sale)

[*Date*]

____
____
____

Dear____________:

This is just a note to let you know I enjoyed meeting you [*at your home*] [*last Friday*].

[*I expect to receive the information shortly that you requested, and will immediately forward it to you.*]

If you have any questions, or if there is any further way I can be of service to you, please don't hesitate to call me.

Yours truly,

____

Thank You for Business

[*Date*]

____
____
____

Dear __________:

Just a note to say Thank You for [*choosing me as your insurance agent*] [*your business*] [*entrusting me with your financial planning*].

All too often in today's rush of business we forget to say "Thanks." I didn't want that to happen.

I have enjoyed filling your needs for [*your homeowner coverage*].

If there is anything further I can do for you, please call on me.

Sincerely,

____

Service Evaluation Form

Please Evaluate—[*Jones Insurance*]

1. Do you feel that the agent asked the proper questions to ascertain your needs?
   [ ] Yes [ ] No [ ] Partially
2. Do you feel that the agent really listened to you so he or she actually understood your needs?
   [ ] Yes [ ] No [ ] Partially
3. Did the agent's recommendations meet your needs?
   [ ] Yes [ ] No [ ] Partially
4. Did the agent fully explain [*the services*] and [*the policy or policies*] you were interested in?
   [ ] Yes [ ] No [ ] Partially
5. Would you recommend the agent to a friend interested in [*insurance coverage, financial services*]?
   [ ] Yes [ ] No

NOTE: *This form shows the client that you are interested in the client and his or her needs. It can be enclosed with a policy of insurance or even a billing. Include a self-addressed stamped envelope.*

Transmittal Letter—Requested Data

[*Date*]

____
____
____

Dear ________:

I have enclosed the information you have requested [*on*] [*concerning*] ______________________________.

I will call you in a few days [*to answer any questions you may have*] [*to get your reaction to this plan*].

Yours truly,

____

Enc.

Transmittal Letter (General)

[*Date*]

____

____

____

Dear __________:

I have enclosed [*an addendum to your automobile policy with Utah Casualty Company*]. [*Please place this (addendum) with your policy.*]

[*If you have any questions at all, please contact me.*]

Yours truly,

____

Enc:

Transmittal Letter—Check for Claim

[*Date*]

____
____
____
____

Re: [*Homeowner Policy #* ____________],
[*Mutual of Sacramento*]

Dear __________:

Enclosed is a check for $__________________ in [*full*] settlement of your claim of [*June 1, 1994*], covered by the above referenced policy [*effective July 1, 1994*].

If you have any questions or if I can be of any additional service to you, please contact me.

Yours truly,

____

Enc: 1

Response to Inquiry—Loan/Cash Surrender Value

[*Date*]

____

____

____

Dear __________:

In accordance with your inquiry, the current [*loan value*] [*cash value*] of your policy number __________ with __________ is $________________.

[*I have enclosed a simple form for you to complete if you wish to (cancel), (borrow on) the above referenced policy.*]

If you have any questions or there is any other way I can be of service to you, please do not hesitate to contact me.

Sincerely,

____

Enc:

Policy Anniversary Letter

[*Date*]

____
____
____

Dear __________:

Today is a very special day. It was [*35 years*] ago that [*we*] [*I*] first wrote [*automobile insurance*] on your [*1959 Studebaker*].

[*We've*] [*I've*] been covering your needs for quite awhile and in case [*we*] [*I*] failed to mention it, thank you for letting [*us*] [*me*] serve you.

[*We*] [*I*] look forward to another [*35*] years of serving your needs.

Yours truly,

____

NOTE: *This is an appropriate letter for 10, 15, 20, etc. years of serving an owner.*

Premium Dollars Equal Cash Value

[*Date*]

____
____
____

Dear __________:

In reviewing your life insurance policy with [*Jones Insurance*], I realized that you have reached the point where the cash value of your policy now exceeds the premiums you have paid to date. Not only will your cash value continue to grow each year at ever-increasing amounts beyond your premium payments, but you will continue to receive the full benefits of $__________________ in life insurance.

I will be calling you in a few days to set up an appointment to review your insurance coverage and to answer any insurance questions you may have.

Yours truly,

____

Term Insurance Conversion

[*Date*]

____
____
____

Dear __________:

It has been [*12*] years since you purchased your $100,000 term life insurance policy with [*United Prudential*]. Term insurance is by far the best choice that a young person can make for family protection. However, our needs change as we get older.

I will be calling you in the next few days to set up an appointment so that you can consider conversion options available that will better serve your present needs.

Yours truly,

____

NOTE: *It isn't necessary at this time to discuss particular products. However, whole life, with higher earnings and cash-value for retirement, would be a likely choice while interest rates are low.*

Increase Life Coverage Available

[*Date*]

____
____
____

Re: Policy No. ____________________

Dear ___________:

Your [*whole life policy*] with [*United Insurance Group*] provides you with [*$35,000*] in coverage.

At the present time we are able to increase this coverage to [*$50,000*] [*without any physical examination*] for an additional premium of [$___________] per month.

I will be calling you in a few days to determine if you wouldlike to take advantage of what I consider to be a favorable opportunity.

Yours truly,

____

Lower Premium

[*Date*]

____
____
____

Dear __________:

I have some good news for you.

Your premium on your [*homeowner's coverage*] with [*Atlantic Mutual*], will be reduced to $____________ for the coming year.

It's really nice to be able to tell someone that costs are going down rather than up.

Incidentally, I will be calling you in a few days to set up an appointment to review your complete coverage package to make certain you are adequately protected at the lowest possible cost.

Yours truly,

____

Enc: Billing

Lower Rate Eligibility

[*Date*]

____
____
____

Dear __________:

Congratulations!

[*You are now (25 years old), (a married person).*] [*It is now (three years) since (your last traffic citation), (your last problem). As you know, this means we can now offer you significantly lower insurance rates.*]

I will be calling you in the next few days to suggest a method whereby these savings can be used to help ensure your future financial well-being.

Sincerely,

____

NOTE: *This letter ties the savings in with an opportunity to sell another product.*

Increased Coverage—No Premium Increase

[*Date*]

____
____
____

Dear __________:

I have some Good News for you.

Your [*personal liability*] coverage on your [*homeowner's policy*] will increase from [*$300,000*] to [*$500,000*] next year without any increase in premium. It isn't often I get to tell someone they're getting something at no additional cost.

[*I will be calling you in the next few days to set up an appointment to review your complete coverage package to make certain you are adequately protected.*]

Yours truly,

____

Enc: Billing

Increase in Coverage and Premium

[*Date*]

____
____
____

Dear __________:

You will notice from the enclosed billing that your ____________________ policy premium has increased slightly from last year. This cost increase is related to the fact that your coverage for ____________ has increased from $____________ to $____________, and ____________________ is now covered by the policy.

[*I will be calling you in the next few days to set up an appointment to review your complete coverage package to make certain you are adequately protected.*]

Yours truly,

____

Enc: Billing

Modification of Coverage/Renewal

[*Date*]

____
____
____

Dear __________:

I want to point out that the renewal of your __________________ policy includes several modifications to your coverage. They include:

1. __________________________________
2. __________________________________
3. __________________________________

I will call you in a few days to answer any questions you may have and to set up an appointment, if needed, to review your present coverage package to make certain you have adequate protection.

Yours truly,

____

Cost-of-Living Adjustment—Disability Income Policy

[*Date*]

____

____

____

Dear ___________:

Your disability income policy with [*Coopers Union*] provides for an annual cost-of-living adjustment. As of [*date*], any disability compensation you may be entitled to shall increase by [*3.2%*].

This cost-of-living adjustment protects the purchasing power of the policy benefits.

I will be calling you in a few days for an annual review of your overall insurance program.

Yours truly,

____

NOTE: *You are using the increased benefit as an opportunity to call regarding an "annual review."*

Adding Variable Annuities to a Fixed Annuity Program

[*Date*]

____
____
____

Re: Policy No. ____________________ with [*Granite Life*]

Dear __________:

The fixed annuity value of your retirement plan now exceeds $____________________.

I will be calling you in a few days to arrange to meet with you [*and your (husband) (wife)*] in order to discuss some alternatives that should increase the yield on your retirement plan. One of several possibilities is to include some variable annuities within the plan.

When I talk with you, I will be able to answer any questions you may have and discuss the options that are available.

Yours truly,

____

NOTE: *Many financial experts feel that a retirement plan should have approximately one-third in market securities for greater equity growth.*

Dividend Reinvestment

[*Date*]

____
____
____

Dear __________:

You will receive a dividend on your Policy No. __________.

I will be calling you in a few days to ascertain if you would like the dividend automatically applied to additional paid-up life insurance coverage. This will increase your insurance as well as your policy loan value without the necessity of paying any additional premiums. I also would like to take the opportunity to review your overall insurance program.

Yours truly,

____

Cost-of-Living Adjustment Rider

[*Date*]

____
____
____

Dear __________:

I am pleased to inform you that a cost-of-living adjustment amendment is now available for your [*Life Policy*] [*Disability Income Policy*] No. ____________________ with [*Granite Life*].

This amendment will provide [*annual*] increases in your insurance coverage based on increases in the [*Consumer Price Index*]. The cost is only $____________ per year. Based on what has happened to costs over the past few decades, I believe this will be a valuable addition to your policy coverage.

I will be calling you in a few days to determine if you desire this low cost additional protection and to take the opportunity to review your overall insurance program.

Yours truly,

____

Disability Income Rider

[*Date*]

____
____
____

Dear __________:

Did you realize that for only $__________ per year we can add a Disability Income Provision to your Life Insurance Policy No. ____________________ with [*Granite Life*]?

This would entitle you to $__________ per month with a limit of $____________________ in the event of a disability prohibiting you from working.

[*If you would like this low-cost addition to your present-coverage, please give me a call.*]

[*I will be calling you in a few days to ascertain your interest in obtaining disability income protection.*]

Yours truly,

____

Accidental Death Benefit (ADB) Rider

[*Date*]

____
____
____

Re: Policy No. ____________________ with [*National City Life*]

Dear __________:

Did you realize that for only $____________ more per year you can [*double*] [*triple*] the amount of your present insurance coverage for accidental death?

With an accidental death benefit rider, death benefits from accidental death under your policy would increase from [*$100,000*] to [*$200,000*] or even [*$300,000*] in certain circumstances.

I will be calling you in a few days to ascertain if you desire this increased coverage.

Yours truly,

____

New Product (Letter to Present Clients)

[*Date*]

____
____
____

Dear ____________:

A [*new program*] [*new financial opportunity*] has become available known as __________________.

I am very excited about this [*program*] [*opportunity*] and I think you might be too! I am enclosing a brief brochure to give you some information.

I will be calling in the next few days to explain why I think this [*plan*] [*opportunity*] will help in fulfilling your [*long-term*] needs.

Sincerely,

____

Enc:

Renewal Discussion

[*Date*]

____
____
____

Dear ______________:

I will be calling in the next few days to discuss your [*homeowner*] insurance policy. The policy comes up for renewal in [*just a few weeks*] and this would be a proper time to make any desired modifications. I have several suggestions that I think will better meet your current needs.

I am looking forward to talking with you.

Yours truly,

____

NOTE: *The purpose of this letter is to let the client understand that you are serving the client's needs and any changes, such as an increase in coverage, will be in the client's best interests.*

Letter to Former Client upon Failure To Renew

[*Date*]

____
____
____

Dear __________:

I was happy to have met your ____________________ insurance needs for [____________ years.] I am troubled when I lose a client whom I have valued.

I will be calling you in a few days to determine if I have failed to meet your needs and if so, in what way. Since my business is built on serving the needs of others, I want to know if there are any ways in which we can restore our relationship or any steps you feel I should take to prevent problems in the future.

Yours truly,

____

Appointment for Physical

[*Date*]

____
____
____________________.

Re: [*Mutual of Nebraska Life Insurance Application*]

Dear __________:

I [*have arranged*] [*am arranging*] for your insurance physical for the [*Mutual of Nebraska*] life policy that we applied for.

Your appointment is:

[*Dr. Sidney Taylor*
Sun Office Center
111 West Vernon Avenue, Suite 608
9:30 A.M.
Thursday, December 12th]

[*You will be contacted by (Doctors Medical Service) to make an appointment for your physical at a time and place that is convenient for you.*]

[*I will have my secretary call you on (December 11th) to remind you of the appointment.*]

Yours truly,

____

Acceptance/After Physical

[*Date*]

____
____
____

Dear __________:

I am pleased to inform you that [*Dr. Stewart*] has given you a clean bill of health.

[*Since you gave me your check for your first premium, you are now covered for ($100,000) in life insurance in accordance with your application.*]

[*Upon receipt of your check for $__________ covering (your first year's premium), your ($100,000) life insurance policy will be in effect in accordance with your application.*]

I think you were wise in choosing this coverage as it perfectly fits your needs and [*protects your family as well as provides for your retirement*].

When the policy arrives from the home office, I will call and make an appointment to deliver it to you in person.

Sincerely,

____

[*Enc: Billing*]

Rated Applicant

[*Date*]

____
____
____

Re: [*Mutual of Oakwood*], [*Life Insurance Application*]

Dear __________:

[*Mutual of Oakwood*] has informed me that they will accept you for [*whole*] life insurance coverage in the amount of $__________________, as requested.

The annual premium for the [*Oakwood Whole Life policy*] is $____________, which is higher than I had quoted.

I will be calling you in the next few days to arrange to discuss the policy offered and alternatives.

Yours truly,

____

Refusal of Application

[*Date*]

____
____
____

Dear __________:

I regret to inform you that [*Mutual of Las Vegas*] has declined to accept your application for [*life insurance*].

[*Enclosed is your premium deposit of $____________.*]

[*Currently, I am making inquiries with other insurers as to obtaining your desired coverage, and I will be contacting you within a few days.*]

If you have any questions, please contact me.

Yours truly,

____

Cancellation Notice

[*Date*]

____
____
____

Re: [*Homeowner Policy No.* ____________________],
[*Mutual of Cedarburg*]

Dear __________:

I regret to inform you that [*Mutual of Cedarburg*] advised me of their cancellation of your [*Homeowner Policy*], [*No.* ____________________], as of [*March 1, 1994*]. [*The carrier did not provide a reason for the cancellation.*] [*The reason given by the carrier for the cancellation was* ____________________.]

[*I have arranged to place your coverage with (North American United) so that you will be fully protected at all times.] [I am attempting to arrange alternative insurance coverage for you and will be contacting you within a few days.*]

If you have any questions please call me.

Yours truly,

____

[*Enc: Billing*]

Cancellation—Nonpayment of Premium

[*Date*]

____
____
____

Dear __________:

We have notified [*Pacific Mutual*] to cancel your [*Homeowner Policy*] No.________________, covering [*address or description*], effective [*this date*] [*date*].

There is a balance owed of $ ________________ covering insurance coverage received until cancellation (as well as cancellation costs). Unless we hear from you by [*date*], we will have to exercise our collection rights.

Sincerely,

____

c.c. [*Mortgagee*]

NOTE: *This letter is final step (see Collection Letters #1 and #2, Pages 198 and 199). Unless the insured party pays the balance or arranges an acceptable payment plan, it is suggested you give the claim to a collection agency. You are not in the collection business so don't waste valuable selling time on collecting small claims.*

Cancellation/Refund of Premium

[*Date*]

____
____
____

Re: [*Homeowner Policy No.* ____________________],
[*Mutual of Los Angeles*]

Dear __________:

Enclosed is a check for $____________ covering the [*short-rate*] [*prorated*] refund of premium based on [*your cancellation*] [*the insurer's cancellation*] of the above referenced policy [*effective July 1, 1994*].

If you have any questions or if I can be of service to you in the future, please contact me.

Yours truly,

____

Enc: 1

Notice of Nonrenewal

[*Date*]

____
____
____

Dear __________:

We have been informed by [*carrier*] that they will not be renewing your [*automobile*] insurance policy No. __________________, which expires on [*date*].

[*I will be seeking alternative coverage for you and will be calling in the next few days to inform you of my progress.*]

[*I suggest that you seek other coverage so that you remain adequately protected. If you have any questions, please contact me.*]

Yours truly,

____

NOTE: *Don't get involved in reasons for nonrenewal.*

Collection Letter #1

[*Date*]

____
____
____

Dear __________:

The premium for your [*homeowner*] policy No. [*67J92374*] in the amount of $____________________ was due on [*date*].

In order for us to maintain your insurance coverage on the above policy, it is necessary that you please forward your payment immediately. Enclosed is a payment envelope.

If there is any problem, I would appreciate receiving your call.

Sincerely,

____

Enc:

NOTE: *It is suggested that a telephone call precede this letter. The call should suggest the client is merely forgetful.*

While this letter does not threaten, it is strong in that cancellation is implied.

Collection Letter #2

[*Date*]

____
____
____

Re: [*Homeowner Policy*] Number ____________________

Dear __________:

The premium for the above referenced policy was due on [*date*] and has not been paid. In addition, we have not received any reply to our letter of [*date*]. Unless we receive payment in the amount of $____________ by [*date*], the above referenced policy shall be cancelled effective [*date*], and appropriate collection measures will also be taken. I very much hope that this action will not be necessary.

Sincerely,

____

cc: [*Mortgagee*]

NOTE: *Don't worry about getting tough with clients who don't pay. Being easy on them could mean failure for you.* *See cancellation letter, page 195.*

NSF Check

[*Date*]

____
____
____

Dear _________:

Your check No.__________, [*copy attached*], has been returned from your bank [*NSF*] [*account closed*].

I realize that you need your [*automobile*] coverage, so I will hold off taking any action on your policy Number _________________, until [*date*]. Unless I have either cash or a Cashier's check in the amount of $__________ in my office by that date, I will have to cancel your [*automobile*] coverage.

If you have any questions, please call me at once.

Yours truly,

____

Enc:

NOTE: *Generally, you should handle an NSF check with a phone call. If you are unable to reach the person, you should use this letter. While you want to show some understanding, you want to make it perfectly clear that you mean business. If payment is not received, follow with cancellation letter (page 195).*

Thank You for a Referral

[*Date*]

____

____

____

Dear __________:

I would like to thank you for [*suggesting that Tom Moore could use my services*] [*recommending me to Tom Moore*].

I was able to meet [*Tom Moore's*] needs and I look forward to a long professional relationship with [*him*].

I am particularly gratified because, by referring me to your friend [*Tom Moore*], you have indicated that I have been able to properly serve your needs, and I will certainly continue to do so.

Again, thank you, and if you have any questions as to your coverage or future needs, do not hesitate to call me.

Sincerely,

____

NOTE: *Consider a handwritten note for greater effect, even though it will take more of your time.*

Request for Testimonial Letter after Claim Settlement

[*Date*]

____
____
____

Dear __________:

I am glad that you feel we were able to handle your recent claim in a prompt and satisfactory manner.

[*It was good that you decided to (include ____________________ coverage) (increase your limits) (reduce your deductible).*]

Many people look at insurance from the negative or premium side rather than as a positive in protection and coverage of losses. Therefore, I would appreciate it if you could send me a short letter telling of the benefits derived from the service I provided.

Testimonial letters from people like yourself are effective in convincing others that it is in their best financial interests to carry adequate insurance [*through an independent agent*].

Thanking you in advance,

____

Request for Testimonial Letter/ Check Transmittal Letter

[*Date*]

____
____
____

Re: Claim No. ____________________ [*United American West Insurance*] No. ____________________

Dear __________:

Enclosed is a check for $__________ in settlement of your claim of [*date*] under the above referenced insurance policy.

I hope you feel the settlement was handled in a prompt and fair manner and look forward to being able to continue to meet your insurance needs.

[*I would like to ask you a favor. If you have a few minutes, write me a short note as to our relationship and claim settlement. Testimonial letters from people like yourself are a powerful tool in convincing others that they should have adequate insurance coverage (with a local independent agent).*]

Sincerely,

____

NOTE: *If you deliver a settlement check to the client, ask for the testimonial letter in person.*

Thank You For Testimonial Letter

[*Date*]

____
____
____

Dear __________:

I would like to thank you for your delightful letter of appreciation as to my services. My [*wife*] [*husband*] says that kind of praise will make me impossible to live with.

All too often, insurance agents are viewed as people trying to sell people something they don't want. It's nice to be regarded as one of the good [*guys*] [*gals*] wearing a white hat and working to help others.

I will do my best to live up to the image you have given me in meeting your insurance needs. I want you to know that I am very proud to be your insurance agent.

All the best,

____

Letter to Client on Newspaper Article about Client

[*Date*]

____
____
____

Dear ____________:

I enjoyed the recent article about you in the [*Journal*]. I have enclosed the article in case you wanted an extra copy.

[*I want you to know I think what you are doing is terrific!*]

Best regards,

____

Enc:1

Client Birthday—Financial Planning

[*Date*]

____
____
____

Dear ____________:

Happy Birthday [*George*]!

You are one year older and one year closer to retirement.

I will be calling you in a few days to review your current financial planning program and to make any applicable suggestions.

Sincerely,

____

Client Birthday

[*Date*]

____
____
____

Dear ____________:

Happy Birthday [*Francis*]!

You're not really getting older, just more experienced. We hope the coming year will offer you experiences of great joy.

All of us at [*Sherman Insurance*] extend Best Wishes to you on your natal day.

____________________ ____________________

____________________ ____________________

____________________ ____________________

Client Marriage/Engagement

[*Date*]

____

____

____

Dear __________:

[*I would like to congratulate you on your recent (marriage) (engagement).*]

[*(I) (All of us at Insure All, Inc.) wish you and (Lawrence) (Cecilia) great happiness in the years to come.*]

[*I would like to congratulate you on the (marriage) (engagement) of your (son) (daughter) (John) (Christine) to (Clarence). I am sure that (Clarence and Sally) will bring you much joy in future years.*]

Very sincerely,

____

Birth of Son/Daughter

[*Date*]

____

____

____

Dear ____________:

Congratulations on the birth of [*Jennifer*]. [*She*] couldn't have chosen two nicer parents.

In a few weeks when things get back to normal, I will call you to discuss various options available for dealing with the greater responsibility that comes with a new child.

Again, I wish the [*three*] of you great happiness.

Best Wishes,

____

NOTE: *This letter would be most effective with the birth of a first child.*

Sympathy

[*Date*]

____
____
____

Dear ____________:

It was with deep sorrow that I heard about the recent passing of your [*husband*] [*George*].

I have known [*George*] [*for many years*] [*for more than* ____________ *years*] and sincerely enjoyed our friendship.

[*I will be contacting you in a few days so that we can prepare the appropriate insurance claim.*]

If there are any questions that you have about any of your insurance coverage, please don't hesitate to contact me.

Yours truly,

____

Christmas Card

May the joyous holiday spirit extend throughout the coming year. Wishing you and yours our very special

Seasons Greetings

from all of us at

[*Johnson Insurance*]

NOTE: *This short season's greetings would be appropriate with a photograph of your staff and families and/or the personal signatures of your staff.*

Chapter 10

Letters of Conflict

Policy Holder Complaint

[*Date*]

____
____
____

Dear ____________:

While I am sorry to hear of your dissatisfaction with [*our services*] [*one of our employees/agents*], I am nevertheless glad that you brought this matter to my attention.

You can be assured that I will investigate your complaint and appropriate action will be taken. [*I am certain that the matter can be resolved to your satisfaction.*]

Yours truly,

____

General Complaint—No Solution

[*Date*]

____

____

____

Dear ____________:

I am very sorry that you have not been satisfied with [*my services*] [*the services of Acme Insurance Agency*]. While it is apparent that [*I*] [*we*] don't always succeed, [*I*] [*we*] nevertheless do strive to meet the needs of our clients. Failures, nevertheless, are important, as they serve to stimulate [*me*] [*us*] to improve.

I want you to know that I would be most happy to meet with you at your convenience to openly discuss this or any other problem you may have.

Yours truly,

____

Complaint—Full Settlement

[*Date*]

____
____
____

Dear ___________:

Re: [*United Prudential Home Owner Policy 73J264*]

In response to your [*letter of June 7*] [*inquiry of June 7*], [*I am*] enclosing a check for $ __________, which covers [*the 17-day delay in our cancellation of your policy as requested*].

I am sorry for any inconvenience caused you. If there is any way I can be of further service to you, do not hesitate to contact me.

Yours truly,

____

Complaint—Settlement Offer

[*Date*]

____
____
____

Dear ____________:

Re: [*General Insurance Group Policy No. 736J4112*]

In answer to your [*letter of July 16*] [*telephone call on July 16*], I am very sorry that you have not been satisfied with our service.

[*While I do not feel that any action by our firm/staff was improper*], I do not want you to remain dissatisfied with our firm. I therefore offer you $ ____________________ in settlement of any claim you may have because of [*your allegations that* ____].

If this is acceptable, please sign the enclosed release and you shall receive the check promptly.

Yours truly,

____

[*Enclosure*]

Release of Claim

[*Date*]

To: [*Clifford Insurance Agency*]

In return for the sum of $ ________________ to be paid me by [*Clifford Insurance Agency*], I hereby waive any rights or claims I may have against [*Clifford Insurance*], its agents, employees or assigns for any acts or omissions arising from [*Homeowner Policy No. X37J21142 with Continental United*].

____

____

NOTE: *This is a sample form only. Seek legal counsel for the preparation of any legal document. Whatever type of release form is used, you will want all persons covered by the policy to sign the release.*

Complaint—Recommendation to Insurer

[*Date*]

____
____
____

Dear ____________:

Regarding [*your letter of November 4*] [*your telephone call of November 4*], I have investigated the problem.

I have recommended to the insurer [*American United Limited*] that [*they rebate $ ____________________ to you as requested because of the dual coverage*] [*they re-adjust the premium to reflect* ____________________].

I hope that this will be satisfactory.

Yours truly,

____

Complaint—Offer To Arbitrate

[*Date*]

____
____
____

Re: [*Your letter of March 1, 1993*]

Dear ____________:

[*I*] [*Acme Insurance*] would like to resolve [____] in a fair and equitable manner. What could be more fair than to submit our disagreement to an impartial arbitrator for binding arbitration? If this appears satisfactory to you, please contact me and we will work out the details of selecting an arbitrator.

[*As an alternative, in the interest of expediency, I would agree to pay you the sum of ($1,000) in full settlement of your complaint.*]

Yours truly,

____

NOTE: *The second paragraph could save you time and money. Sometimes it pays to pay even when you are in the right.*

Answer to Complaint—Legal Inquiry

[*Date*]

____
____
____

Re: [*Claimant or Reference Insured and Policy*]

Dear ____________:

In response to your letter of [*October 17*], we have forwarded a copy of your letter to [*name of carrier*] [*name of law firm*] for their reply.

Yours truly,

____

Forward of Complaint—Legal Inquiry to Law Firm

[*Date*]

____
____
____

Re: [*Homeowner Policy 7G93845*]

Dear ____________:

Enclosed is a copy of a letter dated [*December 15, 1993*], concerning [____________________]. We have notified [*the sender*] that we have forwarded the letter to you for your response.

Yours truly,

____

Enclosure

Official Insurance Inquiry—Complaint

[*Date*]

____
____
____

Re: [*Jim Jones Complaint*]

Dear ____________:

I am in receipt of your letter of [*April 11th*]. I was very surprised that a complaint was made to your office. I have set forth the facts in the enclosure [*and have included signed statements from those involved in this office*].

While I believe the complaint to be entirely without merit, you can nevertheless expect my full cooperation in this matter. If you have any further questions, please do not hesitate to contact me.

Yours truly,

____

Enc: [*3*]

Complaint Resolved

[*Date*]

____

____

____

Dear ____________:

I am pleased that we were able to resolve the problem we had in reference to [________________________]. I hope that the solution is to your complete satisfaction.

If there are any further problems or ways in which we can be of service to you, please contact me.

Yours truly,

____

Chapter 11

Carrier Correspondence

Carrier—Request for Representation

[*Date*]

____
____
____

Dear __________:

[*Our firm is*] [*I am*] interested in representing [*name of carrier*] with the purpose of marketing your line of [*life*] [*medical*] [*casualty*] coverages.

I would appreciate the opportunity to talk with one of your representatives at your earliest convenience.

Yours truly,

____

NOTE: *It is not necessary at this time to give any information about your firm.*

General Transmittal Letter

[*Date*]

____
____
____

Re: [*Homeowner Policy No.* ____________________]

Dear __________:

Enclosed is [______________________________], for [*your immediate action*] [*your information*] [*processing*]. [*Please contact me upon receipt.*]

Yours truly,

____

Status Inquiry

[*Date*]

____
____
____

Re: [____]

Dear __________:

The above referenced [*claim*] [*application*] [*inquiry*] was sent to you on [*March 27*].

What is the present status of this [*claim*] [*application*] [*inquiry*]?

Your prompt attention to this matter would be appreciated.

Yours truly,

____

Complaint—Payment

[*Date*]

____
____
____

Re: [__________________________________]

Dear __________:

[*Please recalculate (your billing No.* ____________*). I believe the correct figure to be ($* ____________*).*]

[*(Ms. Jones), Policy No.*___________________*, received billing dated (July 22), copy enclosed, for $* ____________. *The billing appears to be in error, as (it is over twice the amount of previous billings). Please recalculate this billing and, if correct, forward an explanation for the increase.*]

[*As of this date I have not received payment for Policies* ____
____
____
____________ *(September Commission)*].

Your prompt attention to this matter would be appreciated.

Yours truly,

____

Low Claim Offer

[*Date*]

____
____
____

Re: Policy ___________________, Claim [*No.* ______________]

Dear __________:

My client, [*Tom Smith*], has submitted the above referenced claim. The adjuster, [*Elaine Jones*], has offered [*Mr. Smith*] [*$10,000*], in settlement which [*Mr. Smith*] has declined.

I believe the adjuster's offer, based on the facts as I understand them, to be overly conservative to the point of being bad business. Please reconsider the claim and amend the offer.

It is my hope that a mutually satisfactory solution can be worked out.

Yours truly,

____

cc: [*Tom Smith*]

NOTE: *This letter lets the insured know that serving his or her fair interests is your primary concern.*

Letter to Carrier—Claim Denied/Recommendation

[*Date*]

____
____
____

Re: [____________________], policy [*No.* ____________________]

Dear __________:

[*On August 22*] I submitted a [____________________] claim for [*Mr. Edgar Simmons*] concerning [____________________].

[*On August 22*], [*Mr. Edgar Simmons*] submitted a claim for [____________________]. Your adjuster, [*Harold Hastings*], turned down the claim because [____________________].

I believe that this action was not warranted by either the spirit or the letter of [*Mr. Simmons*]'s policy.

I therefore respectfully request that this action be reviewed.

Yours truly,

____

cc: [*Edgar Simmons*]

Complaint—Failure To Take Action

[*Date*]

____

____

____

Re: [*Jean Chong Fire Loss*], [*Claim XT3743J*]

Dear __________:

[*(On July 13 of this year), I sent you (claim processing forms) requested for (Jean Chong's fire loss).*]

To date, no action has been taken by your office as to this [*claim*]. This is a total of [*72*] days since [*the fire occurred*].

[*My personal reputation has been built on my service to customers. It is therefore of the utmost importance that the carriers I represent promptly and properly service their policies.*]

I expect your prompt response to this problem.

Yours truly,

____

cc: [*Jean Chong*]

NOTE: *Consider addressing letter to company president when you feel the carrier has not handled a complaint properly or in a timely manner.*

Carrier—End of Relationship

[*Date*]

____
____
____

Dear __________:

This is to inform you that we will no longer write insurance for [____].

Please remove our name from your various mailing lists and lists of agents.

Yours truly,

____

Chapter 12

Employee Letters

Employee Transmittal Memo

[*Date*]

____
____
____

Dear __________:

[*Attached*] [*Enclosed*] is [*information I think you will find valuable about a new product being offered by Globe International*].

[*I thought you would like to have this information, as it falls in one of your areas of responsibility.*]

[*After you have had a chance to review this, please let me know so we can see how best to take advantage of it.*]

[*What are your thoughts on its use?*]

[*Initials*]

Notification of Meeting

ATTENTION! ALL AGENTS!

[*Special*] Sales Meeting
[*Monday*]
[*June 17th*] – [*9 A.M. – 10 A.M.*]
at [*Our Office*]
[*To Discuss an Important New Product*]
[*Coffee and Donuts Will Be Served*]
If you cannot attend for any reason, notify
[*John Jones*] at [*423-8324*]

Notification of Training

ATTENTION! ALL AGENTS!

[*Professional Improvement Workshop*]
[*In the Conference Room*]
[*Monday June 1st*]
[*9 A.M. – 12 P.M.*]

[*Tom Lord*] from [*Primary Care Inc.*] will discuss [*new product offerings and successful techniques to emphasize product benefits*].

[*Attendance is mandatory unless excused by* (*Joan Smith*)]

[*If you cannot attend for any reason, notify* (*Joan Smith*)] at [*310-6622*]

Notice to Agent of Missed Meeting

[*Date*]

____

____

____

Dear __________:

You missed a very important [*training session*] *on* [*Monday June 17*] [*as well as our regular staff meeting on (June 21)*]. If there is a problem, I am available to provide any advice or assistance I can.

Because of our importance in the lives of our clients, it is essential that we strive to provide the finest possible service in meeting our clients' needs.

I view these meetings as an important function to aid all personnel. I look forward to your attendance and support in the future.

Sincerely,

____

Complaint Follow-Through

[*Date*]

____
____
____

Dear __________:

I am sorry to say I have received a complaint regarding [____].

[*Could you please meet with me*] [*Could you please meet with me and our attorney*] on [*Friday, May 14*] at [*4 P.M.*] at [*our office*] to discuss the facts involved?

[*I have arranged a meeting between (________________), you and myself at (our office) on (Friday, May 14) at (4 P.M.). If you could come at (3 P.M.), it will give us a chance to get all of the facts straight.*]

Sincerely,

____

Commission/Expense Dispute

[*Date*]

____
____
____

Dear __________:

I would like to meet with you [*and Andrew Smith*] in my office at [*4 P.M.*] on [*April 1*], for the purpose of resolving any disagreement that may exist as to entitlement to [*commission on the policy #* ____________________] covering our client, [*Smith's Machine Shop*].

Sincerely,

____

Employee Congratulations

[*Date*]

____
____
____

Dear __________:

Congratulations on [*your first sale of* ________________] [*your first (million-dollar) policy*] [*exceeding your sales goal for December*] [*being the top salesperson in (our region) in the sale of* (____________________________)].

I hope this accomplishment is merely a prelude to even greater achievements. Use this as just one stepping-stone to the future.

Warmest regards,

____

Employee Recognition/Training Completion or Professional Designation

---

[*Date*]

____
____
____

Dear __________:

You may be justifiably proud of your accomplishments in [*completing the* __________________ *program*] [*attaining the professional designation CLU*]. I know that it wasn't easy, but I am sure the feeling of confidence, prestige within the industry and, most importantly, the ability to serve our clients better makes the time well spent.

Congratulations, not just from me but from our entire [*profession*] [*organization*].

Sincerely,

____

Employee Termination

[*Date*]

____
____
____

Dear __________:

I am very sorry to inform you that [*I*] [*we*] will be unable to retain you as [*an agent with (Thomas Insurance)*].

[*You may pick up your final check at any time during normal business hours.*] [*I will mail you your final commissions as they become due in accordance with your employment agreement.*] It would be appreciated if you could return your office keys and remove your personal belongings.

Please let us know the status of any promises you may have made to policyholders/clients so that we can complete any responsibilities in those areas.

I wish you success in any future endeavors, and if there is any way I can be of help to you, or if you have any questions, please contact me personally.

Sincerely,

____

NOTE: *Normally, this should be handled in a face-to-face meeting. Avoid criticism or any accusations as to honesty, as they could constitute grounds for a libel suit.*

Decline To Hire

[*Date*]

____
____
____

Dear __________:

I want to thank you for considering the [*Thomas Agency*]. [*I was very impressed by your resume.*] [*I was very favorably impressed by our meeting.*]

However, [*there were a number of highly qualified candidates and we decided to hire one of the other applicants*] [*at the present time we are not able to take on additional staff*]. [*I would like to retain your resume in the event our needs change in the future.*] [*I have enclosed your resume so that you can submit it elsewhere.*]

I wish you success in both finding appropriate employment and in your future career.

Yours truly,

____

Employee Birthday

[*Date*]

____
____
____

Dear ____________:

Well, it's been another year. In retrospect it has been a year you can be proud of. You are respected by your fellow [*agents*] [*workers*] as a knowledgeable and caring person. More important, our clients regard you as a true professional who can be relied upon in protecting what they hold dear.

Last but not least, we all regard you as a friend. A very happy birthday, [*George*], from all of us.

______________________	______________________
______________________	______________________
______________________	______________________
______________________	______________________

Letter of Recommendation

[*Date*]

____
____
____

Dear __________:

[*Janet Jones*] worked for the [*Thomas Agency*] from [*August 1968*] to [*the present time*] [*June 1993*] as [*a licensed casualty agent*] [*my personal secretary and assistant*]. [*Janet*] always exhibited the utmost in integrity and a sincere desire to help others.

[*I would hire Janet Jones again without hesitation.*]

Sincerely,

____

Employee Wedding Anniversary

[*Date*]

____
____
____

Dear __________:

My very best wishes to you and [*Michael*] [*Elizabeth*] on your wedding anniversary. As a small token of my personal regard for you I have enclosed [*a certificate for dinner for two at the Biltmore*].

It is my sincere hope that you have a joyful celebration of this and many more anniversaries.

Sincerely,

____

Enc:

Birth of Son or Daughter

[*Date*]

____
____
____

Dear __________:

My warmest congratulations on a miraculous event, the birth of your [*daughter Suzanne*] [*son John*]. Little [*Suzanne*] [*John*] has a [*father*] [*mother*] whom [*she*] [*he*] can be proud of.

This small gift is but a token of my regard for you and the joy I feel with you at this time.

Sincerely,

____

Employee Anniversary with Firm

[*Date*]

____
____
____

Dear __________:

I don't know if you are aware of it, but [*Monday, June 4th*] will mark our anniversary. It will be [*5 years*] since you joined [*The Thomas Agency*].

It has been a time filled with successes and a lot of hard work. You have helped hundreds of families in [*protecting what they have worked so hard for*] [*achieving financial independence*].

I want you to realize that your efforts have not gone unnoticed or unappreciated. I am proud to have you as a part of our firm and look forward to a great many more anniversaries.

Sincerely,

____

Death in Agent's Family

[*Date*]

____
____
____

Dear __________:

I want to offer my sincere condolences to you [*and your son*] on your great loss.

[*Mary*] brought joy to [*her*] family and friends, and [*her*] memory will live on in those whose lives [*she*] touched.

Thinking of you,

____

NOTE: *The above letter could also be handwritten on a condolence card.*

Death of Agent/Employee

[*Date*]

____

____

____

Dear __________:

I wish to offer my personal condolences to you. [*Mary*] [*John*] was a [*licensed casualty agent*] with [*Jones Insurance, Inc.*] for [*7 years*].

[*She*] [*He*] was well liked and respected by all of us as well as by the many clients [*she*] [*he*] aided in meeting their personal needs.

[*Mary*] [*John*] gave unsparingly of [*herself*] [*himself*] in helping others and will be greatly missed by us all.

Sincerely,

____

Chapter 13

Press Releases

Transmittal Letter to Media

[*Date*]

____
____
____

Dear __________:

Enclosed is a press release concerning [*Mr. Frederick Schmidt, who has recently been awarded the Chartered Life Underwriter (CLU) Award*] [*as well as a photograph with caption*]. [*A brochure about the honor earned is enclosed.*]

[*We believe this is a significant achievement deserving of community recognition.*]

If you have any questions or desire further information, please contact me.

Thank you,

____

Enc: [*Photo*], [*Brochure*]

Course Completion

[*John Withers*] Completes Course in [*Small Business Insurance Needs*]

[*John Withers*], an agent with [*Pontiac Insurance Agency of Riverdale*], has recently completed a special course in [*Small Business Insurance Needs*] sponsored by [*United Casualty Insurance*]. This course was designed to enable an agent to analyze the needs of [*small business owners*] and to tailor a program to meet those specific needs.

[*Mr. Withers*] has been with [*Pontiac Insurance*] for [*2 years*]. Prior to joining [*Pontiac Insurance*], [*Mr. Withers*], [*who is a graduate of Iowa State University*], was a [*financial analyst*].

[*Mr. Withers*] lives in [*Orchard Estates*] with [*his wife and two sons*]. [*He is past president of the Clintonville Junior Chamber of Commerce.*]

NOTE: *A glossy 5 × 7 or 8 × 10 photograph of good contrast should be submitted to the local newspaper(s). The caption should be carefully attached to the bottom of the photo with masking tape.*

Professional Designation

[*Theodora Tompkins*] Earns [*CFP*]

[*Ms. Theodora Tompkins*] of [*Clyde Insurance Agency*] in [*Lynwood Heights*] was recently honored by the [*International Association of Financial Planners*], who awarded [*Ms. Tompkins*] the coveted designation [*Certified Financial Planner (CFP)*]. To be eligible for this designation a candidate must complete [a *rigorous course of training and testing*].

[*Ms. Tompkins*] [*has 14 years experience in financial planning*] [*has been associated with the Clyde Agency for 6 years*].

According to [*Ms. Tompkins*], it isn't enough to simply sell a client [a *financial package*] [an *insurance program*]. Today, an agent must understand the specific needs of the client and [*choose the coverage*] [*design a program*] that [*meets these needs*] [*is part of the client's total financial picture*].

[*Ms. Tompkins*] lives in [*Riverdale Heights*] [*with her two daughters*] and is active in community affairs.

NOTE: *This press release should be accompanied by a captioned photograph.*

Sales Award

[*Nina Jones*] Wins Sales Award

[*Clifton Andrews, president of Insure All, Inc. in Emoryville,*] has announced that [*Nina Jones*] [*has been designated*] [*has recently achieved*] [*the Agent of the Year award for 1994*] [*$10,000,000 in financial service products for 1994*] [*the Agent of the Month for January*] [*membership in the exclusive Million Dollar Round Table*].

According to [*Mr. Andrews*], [*Ms. Jones*], who has been associated with [*Insure All, Inc.*] since [*1978*], has established an enviable record of sales of [*financial service products*]. [*Ms. Jones*] credits [*her*] success to "caring about the needs of others and then working to best fulfill those needs."

[*Ms. Jones, who is a graduate of Milton College, lives in Cherry Hill Subdivision with her husband and two daughters. She is a past president of the Cherry Hill Women's Club and is active in church work.*]

NOTE: *Always attach a photograph.*

Promotion/Appointment

[*Insure All, Inc. Has New Sales Manager*]

[*Thomas Little has been appointed (Sales Manager) of Insure All, Inc.*]

[*Mr. Little*] brings a wealth of experience to the position. [*He*] was formerly with [*United Insurance*] as [*Assistant Sales Director*] and has [*a total of 23 years*] of sales experience. [*Mr. Little has been associated with Insure All, Inc. since January.*]

[*Mr. Little, who has the professional designation Chartered Life Underwriter (CLU), has received many honors, including membership in the Million Dollar Round Table for six straight years. He received his bachelor's degree from New York University and his Master's in Business Administration from Stanford University. Mr. Little, his wife Susan (who is associated with the accounting firm of Barham and Bailey), and their two sons reside in Riverdale. Mr. Little is a coach in Little League baseball and is active in Lions and Kiwanis.*]

NOTE: *You could attach a photo of the person promoted or a photo of that person being congratulated by the broker with the appropriate caption.*

New Agent

[*Carlson*] Joins [*Johnson Insurance*]

[*Mr. Richard Carlson*] has recently joined the staff of [*Johnson Insurance at 712 West Main in Riverdale as a general agent*].

[*Mr. Carlson, who is a graduate of the University of Kentucky,*] is licensed to provide [*both life and casualty coverage*] [*a wide range of financial services*]. [*He will, in addition, be specializing in estate and financial planning.*]

[*Mr. Carlson was formerly associated with Clifton Industries in Des Moines as a financial analyst.*] [*Mr. Carlson has had over 12 years' experience in financial planning.*] [*Mr. Carlson has recently completed a comprehensive training program in financial planning.*] [*Mr. Carlson lives in River Heights with his wife Caroline and two daughters. He is past chairman of the River Heights Improvement Association.*]

NOTE: *Always include with press releases a captioned black and white, evenly contrasted glossy photo.*

New Coverage/Representation

Johnson Insurance to Represent Occidental Casualty

[*Johnson Insurance Company, of 172 West Main in Libertyville,*] has been appointed [*a general agent*] for [*Occidental Casualty Insurance*]. [*Occidental Casualty Insurance Company is one of the oldest and most respected names in the insurance industry.*]

According to [*Tom Johnson*], broker, this association will allow [*Johnson Insurance Company*] to offer [*quality casualty coverage tailored to the individual needs of their customers at competitive rates*].

NOTE: *Possibility would be a photo of agent shaking hands in front of office with carrier representation and appropriate caption: [*Keiko Yoshikawa*], left, of [*Occidental Casualty Insurance Co.*], welcomes [*Tom Johnson*], right, of [*Johnson Insurance Co.*], to their family of agents.*

New Owner

New Owners—[*Johnson Insurance Agency*]

[*Mr. and Mrs. Anthony Jones*] have recently purchased the [*Johnson Insurance Agency at 133 West Main in Emoryville*].

[*Mr. and Mrs. Jones, who are both licensed by the State of Illinois in both life and casualty insurance, have a total of over 36 years' experience in the insurance profession. Mrs. Jones has the prestigious Chartered Life Underwriter (CLU) designation.*]

[*According to Mrs. Jones, the agency will continue to offer a full range of insurance and financial services "with the emphasis on service."*]

[*At the present time the agency will continue to do business under the name Johnson Insurance Agency.*] [*The name of the firm has been changed to Jones Insurance Agency.*]

[*Mr. and Mrs. Jones, who now live in Orchard Ridge, formerly lived in Levington, where they were both active in community and charitable activities. They have three children, including a daughter attending Yale University.*]

NOTE: *Be certain to include a photograph. Personal information is important, as it makes the people more real—people whom other people would like to know.*

Office Opening/Relocation

[*Johnson Insurance Opens 2nd Office*]

[*Johnson Insurance Expands*]

[*Johnson Insurance*] has announced [*the opening of an (a second) office in the Murray Building, 136 West 31st Street in Lynnwood*] [*the relocation of its Lynnwood office to the Murray Building at 136 West 3rd Street*].

According to [*Thomas Johnson, President*], the [*expansion*] [*move*] was necessary to better meet the residents' needs of [*Lynnwood*].

The office [*offers full-service life and casualty protection as well as financial planning services*].

NOTE: *Consider a photo of the staff hanging the sign outside the new office, with appropriate caption.*

Epilogue

These letters were prepared to be readily modified to meet just about any need of the insurance professional. They actually serve several purposes. We have included letters that we hope will cover at least 90 percent of your general letter requirements. We have also included solicitation or sales letters. They can save you precious professional time, increase the effectiveness of your communications as well as help you to sell. Keep in mind that solicitation letters, by themselves, are only tools in selling. However, they can be the first step toward a sale. Whenever possible, follow up your letter with a telephone call, which is no longer a "cold" contact. The purpose of the telephone call is not to sell but rather to obtain an appointment. You will then have the opportunity to sell the benefits of your product. Keep your calls brief. Don't use the call to try for a sale. You want to create an interest by which the person called wants more information and is receptive to an appointment.

When you have secured an appointment, end the call. Continued discussion not only wastes time but it also provides an opportunity to cancel the appointment that you have gained. Don't snatch defeat out of the jaws of victory.

If you feel that we have failed to meet a letter need, provided inadequate coverage for an area or have provided inaccurate or misleading letters, please let us know. Write to

William H. Pivar
75-496 Desert Park Drive
Indian Wells, CA 92210-8356

INDEX

A

Accidental death, 77, 78
  dangerous sport, 80
Accidental death benefit (ADB) rider, 186
Achievement, notice to friend/acquaintance on, 17
Affiliation, change of, 15
Agency
  purchase of, 26
  sale of, 25
Agency accounts, purchase of, 27
Agent
  death in family of, 254
  death of, 255
  new, 264
  notice of missed meeting, 242
Anniversary
  employee wedding, 251
  with firm, employee, 253
Annuity, 66–67, 68, 69
  adding variable annuities to fixed annuity program, 192
  flexible-premium deferred, 73
  refund, 72
  split, 71
  tax-deferred, 70
Applicant, rated, 192
Application, refusal of, 193
Appointment for physical, 190
Appointment/promotion, 263
Arbitration, offer of, 221
Audit, insurance, 31, 32
Automobile insurance, 37
  combination homeowner, 98, 102
  dealing with a local agent, 97, 98
  high-risk, 96
  low-cost, 93
  for retiree, 95
  safe driver discount on, 94

B

Benefit package, employee, 159
Birthday
  of client, 206, 207
  of employee, 249
Birth of son/daughter
  of client, 209
  of employee, 252
Blended policy (term/whole life), 54
Boat insurance, 111
Burial life, 43
Business audit solicitation, 141
Business insurance
  general, 142
  specific type business, 143
Business insurance solicitation letters, 141–62
Business interruption insurance, 149–50
Business liability, 154
Buyout insurance, close corporations, 146

C

Cancellation notice, 194
  for nonpayment of premium, 195
  and refund of premium, 196
Career woman
  general insurance for, 36
  universal life for, 61

Carrier, request for representation, 229
Carrier correspondence, 229–36
Cash value, premium dollars equal, 173
Casualty insurance solicitation letters, 93–115
Catastrophic health insurance, 87
Chamber of Commerce, inquiry made to, 20
Charity fundraising through estate planning, 137
Check transmittal letter, 203
Children, whole life for, 50
Christmas card, 211
Christmas season, 23
Claim
  denial recommendation of, 234
  low offer of, 233
  release of, 219
Claim settlement, request for testimonial letter after, 202
Client letters, 165–211
Client referral, 6, 40, 201
Close corporations
  buyout insurance, 146
  disability buyout, 147
Collection letter, 198, 199
Collector's coverage, 110
College fundraising through estate planning, 136
Color, 8
Commission/expense dispute, 244
Company retirement program, 158
Complaints
  answer to, legal inquiry, 222
  failure to take action, 235
  follow-through, 243
  forward of, legal inquiry to law firm, 223
  full settlement of, 217
  general—no solution, 216
  offer to arbitrate, 221
  official inquiry, 224
  payment, 232
  policy holder, 215
  recommendation to insurer, 220
  resolution of, 225
  settlement offer, 218
Computer insurance, 112–13
Conflict, letters dealing with, 215–25
Convertible term insurance, 46
Cost-of-living adjustment, disability income policy, 181
Cost-of-living adjustment rider, 184
Coupons, 7–8
  free, 39
  retirement analysis, 127, 128
Course completion, 17, 260
Coverage
  modification of, 180
  new, 14, 265
  no premium increase and, 178
  and premium increase, 179

D

Dangerous sport, accidental death, 80
Death
  of agent/employee, 255
  in agent's family, 254
Designation, notice to friend/acquaintance on, 17
Director's liability, 157
Disability buyout
  close corporation, 147
  partnership, 145
Disability coverage, key employee, 153
Disability income policy, cost-of-living adjustment, 181
Disability income protection, 82, 83
Disability income rider, 185
Disability overhead expense, 151
Disability solicitation letters, 77–90
Dividend reinvestment, 183

E

Earthquake insurance, 103
800 number, 7
Employee
  anniversary with firm, 253
  benefit package, 159
  birthday of, 249
  birth of son or daughter, 252
  congratulations to, 245
  death of, 255

letters related to, 239–55
recognition/training completion or professional designation, 246
termination of, 247
transmittal memo, 239
wedding anniversary of, 251
End of relationship, 236
Engagement, 208
Estate planning
charity fundraising through, 137
college fundraising through, 136
Estate tax/life insurance, 135
Expense/commission dispute, 244

F

Failure to take action, 235
Fidelity bonds, 156
Financial planning, 119–25
and client birthday, 206
and new parent, 126
Financial products and services solicitation letters, 119–37
Flexible-premium deferred annuity, 73
Floater policy, 114
Flood insurance, 104
Free coupon, 39

G

General insurance solicitation letters, 31–40
Graded-period whole life, 52
Grand opening invitation, 22
Group coverage, nonemployee, 162

H

Health insurance solicitation letters, 37, 77 90
High-risk automobile insurance, 96
Hire, decline to, 248
HMOs, 86
Holiday open house invitation, 24
Home computer insurance, 112–13
Homeowner insurance, 37
combination automobile, 98, 102
expansion of coverage, 101
new purchaser, 100
Hospitalization insurance, 85
Household help, worker's compensation, 115
Hunter's life/disability insurance, 81

I

Individual medical insurance, 84, 86
Industrial life, 43
Inland marine protection, 148
Insurance audit, 31, 32
Insurance profession
letter to friends prior to entering, 11
note to friends (acquaintances) upon entering, 12
Interest-sensitive whole life, 53
IRA, 133

J

Jet ski insurance, 111

K

Keogh Plan, 160
Key employee, disability coverage, 153
Keyperson insurance, 152

L

Landlord policy, 106
Legal inquiry
answer to complaint, 222
forward of complaint, 223
Life insurance solicitation letters, 44–73, 135, 175
Lists, 7
Loan/cash surrender value, 171
Local agent/automobile insurance, 97, 98
Long-term care coverage, 89, 90

Low claim offer, 233
Low-cost automobile insurance, 93
Lower premium, 176
Lower rate eligibility, 177
Low-load universal life, 60

M

Mail advertising, 4–5
Malpractice, 154, 155
Marriage, 208
Media transmittal letter, 259
Medical insurance, individual, 84, 86
Medicare supplemental health insurance, 88
Meeting
  letter after (sale or no-sale), 165
  notice of missed, 242
  notification of, 240
Modified whole life, 52
Mortgage insurance, 47
Motorcycle insurance, 99

N

Neighbor letter, 13
New agent, 264
New coverage/representation, 14, 265
New owner, 266
New parent financial planning, 126
New product (letter to present clients), 187
New purchaser homeowner insurance, 100
New resident, 38
Newspaper article about client, 205
NSF check, 200
Nonemployee group coverage, 162
Nonrenewal, notice of, 197

O

Offer to speak, 19
Office opening/relocation, 16, 21, 267
Open house invitation, 22, 24
Owner, new, 266

P

Parent (new) financial planning, 126
Partnership insurance, 144
  disability buyout, 145
Payment complaint, 232
Personnel handling account, change in, 28
Physical
  acceptance/after, 191
  appointment for, 190
Policy anniversary letter, 172
Policy holder complaint, 215
Premium
  cancellation—nonpayment of, 195
  cancellation—refund of, 196
  increased coverage, no increase in, 178
  increase in coverage and, 179
  lower, 176
Premium dollars equal cash value, 173
Press releases, 259–67
Professional designation, 246, 261
Professional malpractice, 154
Promotion, 263
PPOs, 86
Purchase of agency, 26
Purchase of agency accounts, 27

R

Rated applicant, 192
Rate eligibility, lower, 177
Recognition, employee, 246
Recommendation, 250
Referral. *See* Client referral
Refund annuity, 72
Refusal of application, 193
Relationship, end of, 236
Release of claim, 219
Renew, letter to former client upon failure to, 189
Renewal discussion, 188

Renter's insurance, 105
Representation request, 229
Resident. *See* New Resident
Response to inquiry, loan/cash surrender value, 171
Retiree automobile insurance, 95
Retirement analysis coupon, 127, 128
Retirement plan
  maximization of, 131
  rollover of, 132
Retirement planning, 129, 130
Retirement program, company, 158

S

Safe driver automobile insurance, 94
Sale of agency, 25
Sales award, 262
Sales letters, 3–4
Seminar invitation, 18
Service evaluation form, 167
Settlement, full, 217
Settlement offer, 218
Single person
  general insurance for, 35
  universal life for, 62
Snowmobile insurance, 111
Speak, offer to, 19
Split annuity, 71
Split life, 65
Status inquiry, 231
Supplemental health, 37
Survivorship life, 55
  insurance rates response post card, 56
Sympathy, 210

T

Tax-deferred annuity, 70
Telephone calls, follow-up, 6
  800 number, 7
Termination of employee, 247
Term insurance, 44, 45
  blended policy (term/whole life), 54
  conversion of, 174
  convertible, 46
Testimonial letter, 7
  check transmittal letter, 203
  after claim settlement, 202
  thank you for, 204
Thank you
  for business, 166
  for referral, 201
  for testimonial, 204
Training
  completion of, 246
  notification of, 241
Transmittal letter
  check for claim, 170
  general, 169, 230
  to media, 259
  requested data, 168
Transmittal memo, employee, 239
Traveler insurance, 79
TSA, 134

U

Umbrella policy, 107, 108
Universal life, 57, 58, 59
  career woman, 61
  low-load, 60
  single person, 62
  variable, 63, 64

V

Vanishing-premium whole life, 51
Variable universal life, 63, 64

W

Waterbed insurance, 109
Wedding anniversary, employee, 251
Whole life insurance, 48, 49
  blended policy (term/whole life), 54
  for children, 50
  interest-sensitive, 53
  modified or graded-period, 52
  recently married, 52
  vanishing-premium, 51
Worker's compensation insurance, 161
  for household help, 115